COLLEGE SPELLING

BY

P. B. S. PETERS

PUBLISHED BY

SOUTH-WESTERN PUBLISHING COMPANY

CINCINNATI   NEW YORK   CHICAGO   DALLAS   SAN FRANCISCO

E86

K341
Printed in the United States of America

PREFACE

Words are the tools of speech, and are the means by which we express ideas. This spelling book proposes an indispensable set of working tools essential to the ordinary affairs of everyday activities. In the use of words to express ideas in writing, common sense suggests that these words be correctly spelled.

There is no royal road to becoming a good speller. Spelling is largely a matter of habit, and correct habits in spelling are largely a matter of memory.

It is one of the purposes of this book to assist the learner in acquiring a mastery of the correct order of letters in a word by first presenting the word in ordinary print since visualization is one of the best methods of acquiring knowledge of any kind. The words are then divided into syllables and marked diacritically for proper pronunciation. Correct pronunciation is a valuable aid in determining correct spelling. Brief definitions are given to assist in the proper use of the designated word.

The words in this text were checked with a list of words in common use compiled by Dr. Horn of the University of Iowa, with the idea of forming a "basic writing vocabulary." This research study adds to the authenticity of the list of words used.

The spelling, syllabication, and pronunciation are those authorized in the second edition of *Webster's New International Dictionary*. This revised edition contains many variations from the syllabication of former editions. Thus, *Feb ru ar y, or di nar y, hy giene, war ri or, by laws* were formerly written *Feb ru a ry, or di na ry, hy gi ene, war rior, by-laws*. These are merely illustrative of a number of changes of a similar character.

Human interest is fostered by means of pertinent illustrations following the different lessons. Lessons derived from the names of persons and places and from words that have undergone distinctive changes in meaning also add zest to the study of spelling. The lessons are of uniform length, and each lesson is complete in itself.

In Lessons 167–169 will be found a selected list of new words and old words with new meanings. There are also other lists of special interest which are given more as a matter of general interest than as spelling lessons. They are also useful for reference purposes. Such use may be made of these lists as the teacher finds desirable.

The author acknowledges his indebtedness to Peggie Peters Ave, for her assistance in preparing copy for publication, and in reading proof.

P. B. S. P.

RULES FOR ENGLISH SPELLING

It is impossible to learn to spell by rules alone. The only way to learn to spell is by spelling; and spelling is, in the final analysis, only memorizing. However, there are a few general rules for spelling, with their many exceptions, worth remembering. A knowledge of these rules will often be of material assistance in improving one's spelling vocabulary. The following rules are considered helpful.

Rule 1.—In words ending in final *e*, the *e* is usually dropped on the addition of a syllable beginning with a vowel; as,

hope, hoping	*guide, guidance*	*cure, curable*
judge, judging	*come, coming*	*ride, riding*
force, forcible	*fade, fading*	*use, usage*

Some exceptions:—The *e* is retained in some words for the purpose of correct pronunciation; as,

shoe, shoeing	*dye, dyeing*	*mile, mileage*
singe, singeing	*hoe, hoeing*	*notice, noticeable*

Rule 2.—Final *e* is usually retained on the addition of a syllable beginning with a consonant: as,

move, movement	*late, lately*	*shame, shameful*
peace, peaceful	*hate, hateful*	*safe, safety*
use, useless	*mere, merely*	*pale, paleness*

Some exceptions:

abridge, abridgment	*wise, wisdom*	*true, truly*
judge, judgment	*due, duly*	*argue, argument*

Rule 3.—In words ending in double *e*, both *e*'s are retained before an added syllable; as,

free, freely	*see, seeing*	*agree, agreeing, agreement*

Rule 4.—Words ending in a double consonant retain both consonants on the addition of one or more syllables: as,

ebb, ebbing	*enroll, enrollment*	*full, fullness*
will, willful	*dull, dullness*	*stiff, stiffness*
odd, oddly	*skill, skillful*	*ill, illness*

5

Rule 5.—Words of one syllable, and words accented on the last syllable, and ending in a single consonant preceded by a single vowel, double the final consonant on the addition of a syllable beginning with a vowel: as,

run, running	*begin, beginning*	*drug, druggist*
bag, baggage	*plan, planned*	*prefer, preferred*
wrap, wrapper	*beg, beggar*	*occur, occurrence*

Some exceptions:

refer, reference	*prefer, preferable*	*transfer, transferable*

NOTE: (a) The original word must be a monosyllable or a word accented on the last syllable.

(b) The word must end in a single consonant—not a vowel.

(c) The letters *w* and *y* at the end of words are treated as vowels.

(d) The final consonant must not be preceded by a double vowel or a diphthong.

(e) The added syllable must begin with a vowel.

(f) The letters *h, j, v,* and *w* are never doubled.

(g) The letter *x* is regarded as a double consonant.

(h) The combination *qu* is considered as a consonant.

Rule 6.—Final *y* preceded by a consonant is usually changed to *i* on the addition of a syllable not beginning with *i*: as,

army, armies	*spy, spies*	*busy, business*
enemy, enemies	*ally, allies*	*family, families*

Some exceptions:

shy, shyness	*beauty, beauteous*	*pity, piteous*

Rule 7.—Compounds of *all, well,* and *full* drop one *l*: as,

always, almost	*welfare, welcome*	*fulfill, skillful*

Some important exceptions:
allspice, fullness, and hyphened words; as, *full-fledged*

Rule 8.—Three words, *exceed, proceed,* and *succeed,* end in the sound *ceed*; one word ends in *sede, supersede*; and all other words having this sound end in *cede*; as, *precede, intercede, concede, secede, accede,* and *recede.*

NOTE: *Supersede* is from the Latin *super,* meaning "above", and *sedere* meaning "to sit." This accounts for its spelling.

6

KEY TO PRONUNCIATION

Long Vowel Sounds

ā, as in dāy, māke, lābor.
ē, as in ēve, mēal, serēne.
ī, as in īce, mīle, sīgh.
ō, as in ōar, ōld, bōld.
ū, as in dūe, mūte, tūbe.
ȳ, as in stȳle, mȳ, flȳ.

Short Vowel Sounds

ă, as in ăm, măn, răndom.
ĕ, as in ĕnd, mĕnd, ĕxcuse.
ĭ, as in ĭll, mĭll, admĭt.
ŏ, as in ŏdd, nŏt, tŏrrid.
ŭ, as in ŭp, tŭb, stŭdy.
y̆, as in pity̆, my̆th, busy̆.

OTHER VOWELS AND DIPHTHONG SOUNDS

ã, as in orchãrd.
â, as in âir, câre, pârent.
ä, as in ärm, fär, fäther.
à, as in àsk, gràss, plàster.
ą, as in ąll, tąlk, ląwn.
ạ, as in wạn, whạt, quạlity.
å, as in grådation, våcation.
au (like ô), as in author.
ê, as in êre, thêir, whêre.
ẽ, as in hẽr, gẽrm, makẽr.
ẹ, as in prẹy, obẹy, dẹign.
ĕ, as in ĕvent, dĕpend.
ēē, as in ēēl, knēē, nēēd.
ï, as in pïque, polïce.
ĭ, as in fĭr, bĭrd, shĭrk.

õ, as in dishonõr.
ô, as in ôrb, lôrd, ɛôrk.
ȯ, as in dȯve, ȯther, sȯme.
ọ, as in bosọm.
ǫ, as in dǫ, whǫ, prǫve.
ŏ, as in ŏbey, prŏpose.
ōō, as in ōōze, fōōd, mōōn.
ŏŏ, as in fŏŏt, wŏŏl, brŏŏk.
û, as in ûrge, bûrn, fûrl.
ụ, as in rụde, rụral, intrụde.
ų, as in pųt, fųll, pųsh.
ų̈, as in ų̈nite, formų̈late.
oi, oy, as in oil, boy, toy.
ou, ow, as in out, owl.
ui, as in guile, guide.

MISCELLANEOUS SYMBOLS

ç soft, and s sharp, as in çent, çite, sell, yes.
ɛ hard (like k), as in ɛoɛoa.
çh soft (like sh), as in maçhine.
ġ soft (like j), as in badġe, judġe, ġem.
ḡ hard, as in ḡo, ḡreat, eḡḡ.
ṣ (like z), as in eaṣy, muṣic.

th sharp, as in truth, path.
th flat, as in that, this.
x̱, as in ex̱ist, ex̱ample.
ŋ (like ng), as in bank, linger.
ph (like f), as in cipher, pharmacy.
qu (like kw), as in queen.
tų̈, as in natų̈re, pictų̈re.

NAMES OF DIACRITICAL MARKS

(⁝) suspended bar; (^) circumflex; (¨) dieresis; (˙) dot; (˜) tilde; (ˉ) macron; (˘) breve.

NOTE.—For additional markings see Key to Pronunciation in Webster's Dictionary.

7

THE DICTIONARY

An unabridged dictionary of the English language covers a vast field of encyclopedic information in addition to a comprehensive list of words arranged in an alphabetical order. A dictionary is not merely a spelling book, although it is a reliable authority on correct spelling. A careful study of such a book will reveal the following useful and desirable information:

1. The correct spelling of words.
2. Words that should begin with a capital letter.
3. Compound words or words requiring the use of a hyphen.
4. The proper division of words into syllables.
5. Correct pronunciation by means of diacritical marks.
5. The proper syllables to be accented.
7. The plurals of nouns and the tenses of verbs.
8. Lists of synonyms and homonyms.
9. The development of the meaning of words.
10. Idiomatic meaning of certain words and phrases.
11. Affixes and suffixes—their use and application.
12. The etymology or historical derivation of words.
13. Words that have undergone a change in meaning.
14. A pronouncing gazetteer.
15. A pronouncing biographical dictionary.
16. Foreign words and phrases.
17. A general storehouse of useful information.

CONTENTS

PART 1

Classified Words

"The way to learn to spell is to spell."

Words Common in Business

accrued	ăc cru̱ed′[1]	earned; accumulated; increased.
annul	ăn nŭl′	abolish; make void.
assets	ăs′ sĕts	funds; property in general.
brokerage	brō′ kĕr age (ĭj)	commission paid to a broker.
chargeable	chärge′ à ble	capable of being charged.
collectible	cŏl lĕct′ ĭ ble	payable or exchangeable for value.
committee	cŏm mĭt′tee (mĭt′ĭ)	appointed managing body.
deficit	dĕf′ ĭ çĭt	shortage in an amount.
demurrage	dĕ mûr′ rage (ĭj)	charge made for undue delay.
document	dŏc′ û mĕnt	written evidence or proof.
estimate	ĕs′ tĭ māte	appraise; rate.
fluctuate	flŭe′ tu̱ āte	rise and fall, as prices.
liquidate	lĭq′ uĭ dāte (wĭ)	pay debts or settle accounts.
lucrative	lū′ erà tĭve	gainful; highly profitable.
miscellaneous	mĭs çĕl lā′ nĕ oŭs	consisting of several kinds.
monopoly	mŏ nŏp′ ŏ lў	exclusive control of something.
proceeds	prŏ′ çēedş	amount received from a sale.
property	prŏp′ ĕr tў	that which may be owned.
reasonable	rēa′ şon à ble	fair; within just limits.
remuneration	rĕ mū nĕr ā′ tion[2]	payment for services rendered.
succeed	sŭe çēed′	follow; prosper.
sundries	sŭn′ drĭeş	various small articles or items.
surplus	sûr′ plŭs	amount or quantity left over.
testimonial	tĕs tĭ mō′ nĭ ăl	written recommendation.
vacancy	vā′ căn çў	empty space or gap.

Refer to a dictionary for definition, pronunciation, and use of:
antedate, by-bidder, cartage, restitution, stimulate.

Business is defined as "That which occupies the time, attention, and labor of men for the purpose of a livelihood or profit." *Commerce* has to do with distribution, exchange, and barter, and is narrower in meaning than *business*. An *occupation* may be for either pleasure or business. A *vocation* is a life work, and an *avocation* may be a serious pastime or hobby. The word *business* may be used in a figurative sense; as, "Mind your own business."

---

[1] The silent letter of a double consonant is not indicated.
[2] The syllable "tion" or "sion" is not marked when it has the sound of "shun."

LESSON 2

Words Common in Business

allowance	ăl low′ ănç*e*	portion or amount granted.
arbitration	är bĭ trā′ tion	settlement of disputes by arbitrators.
auxiliary	auˌx ĭl′ ia rў (yȧ)	that which aids or assists.
bankruptcy	băŋk′ rŭpt çў	financial failure leading to discontinuance of business.
collateral	ͼŏl lăt′ ēr ăl	stocks pledged as security.
coupon	ͼoụ′ pŏn	interest note or certificate.
dissolution	dĭs sŏ̇ lū′ tion	termination of a relationship.
efficiency	ĕf fi′ cien çў (fĭsh)	skill or competence.
indebtedness	ĭn dĕ*bt*′ ĕd nĕss	amount due or owed.
indemnity	ĭn dĕm′ nĭ tў	protection against loss.
insolvent	ĭn sŏl′ vĕnt	unable to pay one's debts.
license	lī′ çĕns*e*	legal permit to do something.
management	măn′ag*e* mĕnt (ĭj)	administration; government.
merchandise	mēr′ chăn dīṣ*e*	goods used in commerce.
nominal	nŏm′ ĭ năl	existing in name only.
owing	ō*w*′ ĭng	due, as a debt.
patron	pā′ tròn	regular customer.
postdate	pōst dāt*e*′	date in advance.
prosperous	prŏs′ pēr oǔs	financially successful.
receiver	rě çē*i*v′ ēr	officer in charge of property.
retail	rē′ tā*i*l	sell in small quantities.
retrench	rě trĕnch′	cut down cost or expenses.
statement	stāt*e*′ mĕnt	summary; report; account.
transaction	trăns ăe′ tion	business deal.
ultimo	ŭl′ tĭ mō	in the preceding month.

Refer to a dictionary for definition, pronunciation, and use of:

expedite,   franchise,   measure,   subsidy,   voucher.

The English word *bankrupt* is derived from *banca rotta*, an Italian word meaning "a broken bench or bank." In early times in Italy money-lenders used to display the money they had available for loans on a bench. If for any reason the lender was unable to continue in business, his bench was broken and he was termed a bankrupt.

14

Words Common in Business

appraisement	ăp prāi̯se̯′ mĕnt	estimated value of property.
competition	eŏm pĕ tĭ′ tion	rivalry.
complaint	eŏm plāint′	grievance.
concern	eŏn çẽrn′	firm and its business.
concession	eŏn çĕs′ sion	grant or right; thing yielded.
countersign	eoun′ tẽr sīgn	additional signature.
defray	dĕ frāy′	pay; provide for payment of.
discrimination	dĭs erĭm ĭ nā′ tion	unfair difference.
enterprise	ĕn′ tẽr prī̯se̯	undertaking; venture.
exports	ĕx′ pōrts	commodities sent abroad.
fiscal	fĭs′ eăl	financial.
fraudulent	fraud′ u̯ lĕnt (frôd)	guilty of trickery; deceitful.
implied	ĭm plīed′	understood, but not expressed.
integrity	ĭn tĕg′ rĭ tў	uprightness; honesty.
invoice	ĭn′ voiçe	written statement of goods.
kiting	kīt′ ing	exchanging checks for credit.
manufactory	măn u̯ făe′ tŏ rў	place where goods are made.
possession	pŏs ses′ sion (zĕsh)	ownership; control; hold.
proprietor	prŏ prī′ ĕ tŏr	owner of a business.
purchasable	pûr′ chas ȧ ble (chĭs)	capable of being bought.
recommend	rĕe ŏm mĕnd′	speak in favor of; commend.
renewal	rĕ new′ ăl	extension of time or credit.
statistics	stȧ tĭs′ tĭes	assembled, classified facts.
stipulation	stĭp u̯ lā′ tion	agreement; bargain.
wealthy	wĕalth′ ў	affluent; moneyed.

Refer to a dictionary for definition, pronunciation, and use of:

corporation, dispatch, petition, schedule, superscribe.

Many words in common use today may have been ordinary slang at one time. The word *salary* is derived from the Latin *salarium*, meaning "salt-money," the money which was given to Roman soldiers for salt was part of their pay. This may be the origin of the expression "He is not worth his salt."

Spilling salt was considered an unlucky omen by the Romans. The superstition has descended to the present generation.

Words Common in Business

accuracy	ăe′ e̊ŭ rȧ çўˇ	freedom from mistakes.
appraise	ăp prāi̱s̱e′	estimate; fix the value of.
association	ăs sō çı̆ ā′ tion	organized group or body.
commerce	eŏm′ mĕrçe	trade; business in general.
compromise	eŏm′ prŏ mī̱s̱e	settlement by mutual concessions.
consolidate	eŏn sŏl′ ı̆ dāte	unite into one body.
contraband	eŏn′ trȧ bănd	trade forbidden by law.
dealer	dēal′ ẽr	one engaged in business.
industry	ı̆n′ dŭs trўˇ	branch of business, occupation, or trade.
interest	ı̆n′ tẽr ĕst	payment for the use of money.
margin	mär′ gı̆n	amount in reserve.
parcel	pär′ çĕl	small bundle or package.
remittance	rĕ mı̆t′ tănçe	money sent in payment.
rescind	rĕ scı̆nd′	revoke; annul or cancel.
revenue	rĕv′ ĕ nūe	income from any source.
salary	săl′ ȧ rўˇ	money paid for services.
shrinkage	shrı̆ŋk′ age (ı̆j)	depreciation in value.
specimen	spĕç′ ı̆ mĕn	sample; pattern; model.
syndicate	sўˇn′ dı̆ eăte	combination of capitalists.
tacit	tăç′ ı̆t	understood or implied.
telegram	tĕl′ ĕ grăm	message sent by telegraph.
temporary	tĕm′ pŏ rar ўˇ (rĕr)	transient, not permanent.
transcribe	trăn serībe′	make a copy in writing.
usury	ū′ su rўˇ (zhŏŏ)	excessive or illegal interest.
value	văl′ ūe	real worth; market price.

Consult a dictionary for definition, pronunciation, and use of:

allotment,   ratify,   revocation,   technique,   zealous.

A word is *obsolescent* when it wears out gradually or falls into disuse. It may be revived later for adding novelty to an expression: as, "Ye Olde Tea Shoppe," and as a result may regain position for a time. A word is *obsolete* when it is no longer in use; as, *forgat, holpen, meseems, yclept.*

Red tape refers to a strict adherence to official routine. It is so-called from the custom of tying law papers with red tape.

Words Common in Business

accomplish	ăe ĕŏm′ plĭsh	achieve; complete; perform.
administer	ăd mĭn′ ĭs tẽr	direct or superintend; manage.
appraisal	ăp prāĭş′ ăl	valuation of property.
average	ăv′ ẽr ag*e* (ĭj)	arithmetical mean; ordinary; typical.
bankrupt	băŋk′ rŭpt	one who fails in business.
bonanza	bŏ năn′ zȧ	anything highly profitable.
bonus	bō′ nŭs	extra payment as a premium.
boycott	boy′ eŏtt	refuse to have dealings with.
business	bus*i*′ nĕss (bĭz′)	traffic or trade, in general.
commend	eŏm mĕnd′	recommend as worthy of notice.
concur	eŏn eûr′	agree or unite in action.
confidential	eŏn fĭ dĕn′ tial (shăl)	private; trustworthy.
consignee	eŏn sīgn ēē′	one to whom goods are shipped.
deposit	dĕ pŏş′ ĭt	money placed in a bank.
dunning	dŭn′ nĭng	urging payment of a debt.
efficient	ĕf fĭ′ cient (shĕnt)	capable; competent; able.
genuine	gĕn′ ŭ ĭn*e*	real; not counterfeit.
guaranty	gŭăr′ ăn tў	security against loss.
installment	ĭn stąll′ mĕnt	part payment of a debt.
itemized	ī′ tĕm īz*e*d	detailed.
outlawed	out′ ląw*e*d	deprived of protection of law.
profitable	prŏf′ ĭt ȧ bl*e*	yielding a gain or benefit.
solicit	sŏ lĭç′ ĭt	ask with earnestness.
supervise	sū pẽr vīş*e*′	oversee and direct; superintend.
warranty	wąr′ răn tў	guarantee of title or quality.

Consult a dictionary for definition, pronunciation, and use of:

mercantile,   requisite,   summary,   valid,   wages.

Argot is the slang that is peculiar to any class or group, especially that of thieves and rogues: as, *hoosgow* for *jail*; *icebox* for *safe*; *typewriter* for *machine-gun*; *pineapple* for *bomb*; *mouthpiece* for *lawyer*.

Star Chamber was a former English court having jurisdiction over offenses chiefly against the Crown. It was abolished three centuries ago.

LESSON 6

Words Common in Business

accumulate	ăe eū′ mŭ lāt*e*	store up; gather.
assignment	ăs sī*g*n′ mĕnt	written transfer of title.
borrower	bŏr′ rŏ*w* ẽr	one who obtains a loan.
chattel	chăt′ t*e*l	movable personal property.
commission	eŏm mĭs′ sion	allowance for services.
commodity	eŏm mŏd′ ĭ tў	any article of trade.
customer	eŭs′ tŏm ẽr	regular buyer or dealer.
defalcation	dē făl eā′ tion	misappropriation of money.
dishonest	dĭs *h*ŏn′ ĕst	corrupt; deceitful.
dormant	dôr′ mănt	sleeping; temporarily inactive.
embargo	ĕm bär′ gō	prohibition put on commerce.
establish	ĕs tăb′ lĭsh	place on a permanent basis.
expert	ĕx′ pẽrt	one possessing special skill.
extension	ĕx tĕn′ sion	postponement of payment.
industrious	ĭn dŭs′ trĭ o*ŭs*	busy; perseveringly active.
organization	ôr găn ĭ zā′ tion	united group of persons.
package	pă*ck*′ ag*e* (ĭj)	bundle of articles; parcel.
partner	pärt′ nẽr	associate in business.
payable	pā*y*′ à bl*e*	justly due.
preparation	prĕp à rā′ tion	process of making ready.
punctual	pŭŋe′ t*ŭ* ăl	prompt.
receivable	rĕ çēiv′ à bl*e*	due or callable.
rectify	rĕe′ tĭ fȳ	right a wrong.
resources	rĕ sō*ur*′ çĕ*ş*	available means of any kind.
speculator	spĕe′ *ŭ* lā tŏr	one engaged in risky deals.

Consult a dictionary for definition, pronunciation, and use of:

credentials,   discrepancy,   eligible,   recompense,   supply.

A silent letter is one not intended to be heard when a word is properly pronounced; as, *almond, balm, column* (not *colyum*), *gnarled, league, mortgage, pneumonia, ptomaine, wrestle, writhe.*

Apollo was the son of Jupiter and Latonia. He was known as the god of music, poetry, eloquence, medicine, and the fine arts.

Lien at one time meant a ligament or band for binding. Now it has reference to a claim on property of another for payment of a debt.

LESSON 7

Words Common in Business

arrears	ăr rēarṣ′	behind in payment.
capitalist	eăp′ ĭ tăl ĭst	man of considerable wealth.
cashier	eăsh *i*ēr′	one who has charge of money.
certified	çĕr′ tĭ fīed	guaranteed, as a check.
clientele	elī ĕn tĕl*e*′	body of patrons; clients.
counterfeit	eoun′ tĕr f*e*ĭt	illegal imitation of money.
currency	eûr′ rĕn çў	medium of exchange.
debenture	dĕ bĕn′ tўr*e*	bond issued by a corporation.
defaulter	dĕ fault′ ĕr (fôl)	embezzler; one delinquent.
depositor	dĕ pŏṣ′ ĭ tŏr	one who puts money in a bank.
dishonor	dĭs *h*ŏn′ ŏr	fail or refuse to pay, as a note.
exchange	ĕx chānġ*e*′	barter or traffic; trade.
financier	fĭn ăn çī̆ēr′	one skilled in money matters.
hypothecate	hȳ pŏth′ ĕ eāt*e*	give or pledge as security.
investment	ĭn vĕst′ mĕnt	source of income or profit.
negotiable	nĕ gō′ ti ȧ bl*e* (shĭ)	transferable; assignable.
negotiate	nĕ gō′ ti āt*e* (shĭ)	come to terms.
nickel	nĭck′ ĕl	small coin; five-cent piece.
operator	ŏp′ ĕr ā tŏr	dealer in stocks and bonds.
option	ŏp′ tion	right or power to choose.
promoter	prо̑ mōt′ ĕr	organizer of a company.
savings	sāv′ ĭngṣ	sums saved from time to time.
securities	sĕ eū′ rĭ tĭ*e*ṣ	certificates, stocks or bonds.
specie	spē′ cie (shĭ)	coin, usually gold or silver.
teller	tĕll′ ĕr	clerk who handles money.

Consult a dictionary for definition, pronunciation, and use of:

barter, defunct, exhibition, expensive, treasurer.

The same word may have several different meanings, or may be used as two or more different parts of speech. When you look up the definition of an unfamiliar word, ascertain the meaning that fits into the sentence in which the word is to be used. How many different meanings does the word *fast* have?

The word *candidate* literally means "one who wears white." A Roman candidate for office wore a white toga to signify his purity of purpose.

Office Supplies and Equipment

LESSON 8	LESSON 9	LESSON 10
addressograph	envelopes	protector
adhesive	equipment	puncher
appliances	eradicator	records
baskets	erasers	registers
billheads	fasteners	ribbons
binders	files	rulers
blotters	fixtures	scales
brushes	folders	sharpener
buzzer	hectograph	shears
cabinets	index	sponges
calculator	labels	stamper
carbon	letterheads	staples
catalog	lockers	stencils
chairs	mailer	stylus
clips	mimeograph	supplies
clock	moistener	tables
comptometer	mucilage	tablets
copyholder	multigraph	tabulator
covers	paper	telephone
desks	paste	tickets
diaries	pencils	ticklers
dictaphone	perforator	tubes
directory	portfolio	typewriters
duplicator	postage	utensils
duster	protectograph	wrappers

Refer to a dictionary for definition, pronunciation, and use of:

atlas,   facsimile letters,   loose-leaf devices,   manifolding.

Stationery refers to articles usually sold by a stationer; as, paper, ink, pencils, blank books, and other articles used in writing.

A *stationer* originally occupied a station or stall in the market place.

Stationary means fixed in one place, not moving or appearing to move; stable; not changing.

Mercury was the son of Jupiter and Maia. He was the messenger of the gods, the inventor of letters, and the god of commerce.

LESSON 11

Words Pertaining to Law

administrator	ăd mĭn′ ĭs trā tŏr	one who manages an estate.
agreement	à grēē′ mĕnt	legal document; mutual promise.
alimony	ăl′ ĭ mō nў	divorced wife's allowance.
claimant	elāim′ ănt	one who asserts his rights.
codicil	eŏd′ ĭ çĭl	short addition to a will.
consideration	eŏn sĭd ĕr ā′ tion	inducement for making a contract.
decree	dĕ eree′	legal order; judicial decision.
demur	dĕ mûr′	object; take exceptions.
evidence	ĕv′ ĭ dĕnçe	facts; proof; testimony.
executor	ĕx ĕe′ û tŏr	testator's representative.
guardian	guärd′ ĭ ăn	one who has charge of another.
jurisdiction	jц rĭs dĭe′ tion	extent of official authority.
libel	lī′ bĕl	written defamatory statement.
minor	mī′ nŏr	one who is not of legal age.
negligence	nĕg′ lĭ ġĕnçe	lack of care; heedlessness.
probate	prō′ bāte	official proof of a will.
replevin	rĕ plĕv′ ĭn	lawful recovery of property.
sheriff	shĕr′ ĭff	chief county peace officer.
tort	tôrt	civil wrong or injury.
trespass	trĕs′ pàss	intrude on another's land.
validity	và lĭd′ ĭ tў	legal sufficiency.
venue	vĕn′ ūe	place where a trial is held.
verbal	vĕr′ băl	oral; consisting merely of words.
verdict	vĕr′ dĭet	decision reached by a jury.
wrong	wrŏng	injustice.

Refer to a dictionary for definition, pronunciation, and use of:

bailiff, clemency, conciliate, inherit, malice.

A *shyster* is a lawyer who carries on a legal business in a dishonorable way. He is a legal trickster.

There is a United States statute making it illegal to write a check for less than one dollar.

In Michigan a justice of the peace is forbidden to hold court in a barroom.

Words Pertaining to Law

actionable	ăe′ tion à ble	affording grounds for a suit.
adjudge	ăd jŭdge′	decide, as a judge.
adjudicate	ăd ju̱′ dĭ eāte	settle by judicial decree.
attachment	ăt tăch′ měnt	act of taking into custody.
attorney	ăt tor′ neў (tûr)	lawyer; legal representative.
confirmation	eŏn fĭr mā′ tion	act of making sure; proof.
escrow	ěs erō*w*′	sealed instrument held in trust.
executory	ěx̱ ĕe′ ŭ tō rў	designed to be executed later.
falsify	fạl′ sĭ fȳ	alter; prove to be untrue.
incompetency	ĭn eŏm′ pĕ těn çў	lack of proper qualifications.
invalid	ĭn văl′ ĭd	void; null
legacy	lĕg′ à çў	gift of property by a will.
legal	lē′ gă̆l	lawful; according to law.
mandamus	măn dā′ mŭs	command from a superior court.
notary	nō′ tà rў	one who attests legal papers.
precedent	prĕç′ ē̆ děnt	authority followed in courts.
protest	prŏ těst′	make a formal objection.
quash	qua̱sh	set aside; make void.
slander	slăn′ děr	false and malicious report.
statute	stăt′‿ūte	enacted written law.
surety	su̱re′ tў	bondsman for another.
testator	těs tā′ tŏr	one who makes a will.
testimony	těs′ tĭ mō nў	proof; evidence; deposition.
voidable	void′ à ble	capable of being annulled.
waiver	wāi*v*′ ĕr	relinquishment of a right.

Refer to a dictionary for definition, pronunciation, and use of:

curtesy, alienate, foreclosure, ratification, validate.

A *pettifogger* is a lawyer who deals in petty cases. He is an inferior lawyer given to quibbling.

In Scranton pointed fence pickets are illegal.

It is illegal in Maryland for a wife to rifle her husband's pockets while he is asleep.

22

Words Pertaining to Law

abeyance	a̯ bey̯' ănçe	temporary inactivity; expectancy.
accuse	ăe eūṣe'	charge with wrongdoing.
action	ăe' tion	suit at law; legal proceedings.
affidavit	ăf fĭ dā' vĭt	written statement under oath.
annulment	ăn nŭl' mĕnt	abolition; invalidation.
arraign	ăr rāign'	accuse before a court.
attest	ăt tĕst'	bear witness by a signature.
breach	brēach	violation of an obligation.
charter	chär' tēr	written grant or privilege.
client	elī' ĕnt	one who consults a lawyer.
coverture	eȯv' ēr t̯u̯re	status of a married woman.
defendant	dĕ fĕnd' ănt	one sued at law.
defense	dĕ fĕnse'	act of defending.
duress	dū' rĕss	actual or threatened violence.
ejectment	ĕ jĕet' mĕnt	expulsion; dispossession.
exemption	ĕx̱ ĕmp' tion	freedom from a duty.
incorporate	ĭn eȯr' pŏ rāte	form as a legal body.
incriminate	ĭn erĭm' ĭ nāte	charge with a crime or fault.
injunction	ĭn jŭn̯e' tion	judicial order or decree.
litigant	lĭt' ĭ gănt	one engaged in a lawsuit.
malpractice	măl prăe' tĭçe	improper medical treatment.
prosecute	prŏs' ĕ eūte	bring a legal action against.
rebuttal	rĕ bŭt' tăl	formal contradiction.
redemption	rĕ dĕmp' tion	recovery; restoration.
repeal	rĕ pēal'	recall or revoke a statute.

Refer to a dictionary for definition, pronunciation, and use of:

appellant,   complaint,   deposition,   docket,   penal.

Los Angeles has a law forbidding the bathing of two babies in a single bathtub at one time.

In Portsmouth, Ohio, ball players are classified as vagrants, beggars, thieves, and other suspicious characters. They are subject to fine or imprisonment if unable to give a reasonable account of themselves.

Words and feathers the wind carries away. — HERBERT.

Railroading and Transportation

baggage	băg′ gage (ĭj)	trunks; valises; suitcases.
caboose	ҽȧ bōōse′	car used by the train crew.
carload	eär′ lōad	load that fills a car.
classification	ҽlăs sĭ fĭ ҽā′ tion	act of arranging in groups.
collision	ҽŏl lĭ′ sion (lĭzh)	coming together with force.
conductor	ҽŏn dŭe′ tŏr	one in charge of a train.
drawback	draw′ băck (drô)	rebate from regular charges.
engineer	ĕn ğĭ nēēr′	operator of an engine.
interurban	ĭn tēr ûr′ băn	between cities or towns.
junction	jŭ ̧ŋe′ tion	place where roads meet.
locomotive	lō ҽŏ mō′ tĭve	engine for drawing cars.
mileage	mīle′ age (ĭj)	distance in miles.
passenger	păs′ sĕn ğĕr	one traveling in a conveyance.
railway	rāi̯l′ wāy	line of rails or tracks.
route	route (rōōt)	line of march or travel; road.
signal	sĭg′ năl	sign conveying information.
tariff	tăr′ ĭff	classified list of rates.
terminal	tēr′ mĭ năl	end of a railroad line.
tonnage	tȯn′ nage (ĭj)	freight-carrying capacity.
tourist	tou̯r′ ĭst	one who travels for pleasure.
trackage	trăҽk′ age (ĭj)	railroad tracks collectively.
traffic	trăf′ fĭe	business done on a railway.
transportation	trăns pŏr tā′ tion	conveyance; removal.
traveler	trăv′ ĕl ēr	one who goes on a journey.
voyage	voy′ age (voi′ ĭj)	journey by sea or water.

Refer to a dictionary for definition, pronunciation, and use of:

cargo,   **coupler,**   **intrastate,**   **train dispatcher.**

In many parts of the United States, the word *route* is pronounced "rout" (the *ou* having the sound of *out*), but this is now considered as being somewhat provincial. The better pronunciation is "root."

The word *privilege* is a tricky word to spell. Note that the word contains two *i*'s and two *e*'s, but no *a* or *d*.

Minerva was the goddess of wisdom, the arts, and war. She was born from Jupiter's head.

Railroading and Transportation

blockade	blŏck āde′	obstruction to passage.
breakage	breāk′ age (ĭj)	allowance for things broken.
carriage	eăr′ rĭage	wheeled vehicle for conveyance of persons.
carrier	eăr′ rĭ ẽr	one engaged in carrying.
depot	dē′ pōt	railroad station; warehouse.
destination	dĕs tĭ nā′ tion	place to which one is going.
differential	dĭf fẽr ĕn′ tial (shăl)	difference between rates.
dispatcher	dĭs pătch′ ẽr	one who sends messages.
en route	en rọute′ (än)	on or along the way or road.
excursion	ĕx eûr′sion (zhŭn)	pleasure trip.
express	ĕx press′	rapid means of conveyance.
forward	fôr′ wārd	send or ship outward.
lading	lād′ ĭng	loading; cargo; freight.
limited	lĭm′ ĭ tĕd	restricted to a certain class or number.
luggage	lŭg′ gage (ĭj)	trunks, packages, or baggage.
navigation	năv ĭ gā′ tion	naval science.
prepay	prē pāy′	pay the charges in advance.
rebate	rē′ bāte	deduction from sum paid.
salvage	săl′ vage (ĭj)	that which is saved from loss.
shipper	shĭp′ pẽr	person who ships goods.
steerage	stēēr′ age (ĭj)	cheaper quarters on a ship.
truckage	trŭck′ age (ĭj)	movement of goods by truck.
tunnel	tŭn′ nĕl	underground passageway.
vehicle	vē′ hĭ ɇle	means of conveyance.
wreck	wrĕck	break up or shatter.

Consult a dictionary for definition, pronunciation, and use of:

drayage, interstate, manifest, survey, transit.

The word *journey* originally meant "a day's travel." It now refers to travel without regard to time or distance. The word comes to us through the Latin *diurnalis—diurnal—*meaning "daily." From this source we get *journal* used in bookkeeping, or as a newspaper or a diary.

LESSON 16

Words Associated with Insurance

accumulation ăe eū mŭ lā′ tion that which has been saved.
actuary ăe′ tụ ar ў (ĕr) expert computer of insurance risks.
ancestry ăn′ çĕs trў birth or line of descent.
arson är′ son illegal burning of a building.
beneficiary bĕn ĕ fi′ ci ar y receiver of the benefits.
(fĭsh′ ĭ ĕ rĭ)
cancel eăn′ çĕl revoke; mark or strike out.
casualty eas′ ū ăl tў (kăzh)serious or fatal accident.
contributory eŏn trĭb′ ū tō rў giving or lending aid.
convertible eŏn vẽrt′ ĭ ble interchangeable.
damage dăm′ age (ĭj) harm; loss due to an injury.
disability dĭs à bĭl′ ĭ tў incapacity; lack of ability.
dividends dĭv′ ĭ dĕndṣ profits paid to policyholders.
endowment ĕn dow′ mĕnt sum payable at a fixed period.
forfeiture fôr′ fei tụre penalty for failure to act.
fraternal frà tẽr′ năl organized for mutual benefit.
hazardous hăz′ ärd oŭs risky; dangerous.
immunity ĭm mū′ nĭ tў freedom from any charge.
inadequate ĭn ăd′ ĕ quate (kwĭt) insufficient; deficient.
insurance ĭn sur′ ănçe indemnity against loss.
(shŏŏr)
loading lōad′ ĭng amount added for expenses.
policy pŏl′ ĭ çў contract of insurance.
reimburse rē ĭm bûrse′ refund; repay; pay back.
suicide sū′ ĭ çĭde self-destruction; self-murder.
survivor sur vĭv′ ōr (sẽr) one who outlives another.
suspension sŭs pĕn′ sion stoppage of activity.

Refer to a dictionary for definition, pronunciation, and use of:

adjuster,   income,   maturity,   minimum,   security.

The term *assurance* at one time related to contracts of insurance. It is still quite commonly used in connection with English companies engaged in the insurance business.

A *twister* is an agent who tries to induce a policyholder to drop his present policy and substitute another. Such an act is called a *twist*, in the insurance business.

Words Associated with Insurance

adjustment	ăd jŭst′ mĕnt	determination of amount due.
annuity	ăn nū′ ĭ tў	annual allowance or income.
anticipation	ăn tĭç ĭ pā′ tion	expectancy of life.
assessment	ăs sĕss′ mĕnt	share of expenses.
certificate	çĕr tĭf′ ĭ ƈate (kĭt)	written or printed statement.
contingency	ƈŏn tĭn′ ġĕn çў	possible event.
duration	dŭ rā′ tion	length of time.
equitable	ĕq′ uĭ tȧ ble (wĭ)	impartial; just; reasonable.
expectation	ĕx pĕe tā′ tion	prospect of the future.
incendiary	ĭn çĕn′ dĭ ar ў (ĕr)	one who maliciously burns property.
incontestable	ĭn ƈŏn tĕst′ ȧ ble	undeniable; certain.
indispensable	ĭn dĭs pĕn′ sȧ ble	absolutely necessary.
industrial	ĭn dŭs′ trĭ ăl	refers to a type of insurance.
inflammable	ĭn flăm′ mȧ ble	easily taking fire; combustible.
insurable	ĭn sur′ ȧ ble (shŏŏr)	capable of being protected.
insurant	ĭn sur′ ănt (shŏŏr)	one who takes out insurance.
lapse	lăpse	cease, as insurance.
liability	lī ȧ bĭl′ ĭ tў	quality of being responsible.
longevity	lŏn ġĕv′ ĭ tў	long duration of life.
mortality	môr tăl′ ĭ tў	death rate in a given time or in a given community.
mutual	mū′ tu̱ ăl	owned by the policyholders.
premium	prē′ mĭ ŭm	sum paid for insurance.
representation	rĕp rĕ s̱ĕn tā′ tion	statement of fact.
reserve	rĕ s̱ĕrve′	accumulated funds or assets.
underwriter	ŭn′ dĕr ᴡrīt ĕr	company writing insurance.

Refer to a dictionary for definition, pronunciation, and use of:

fidelity,   maximum,   peril,   protection,   risk.

Graveyard insurance is a term applied to a method of swindling insurance companies. One in robust health is substituted for an old or infirm person in the medical examination.

A *binder* is a temporary receipt issued to protect the policyholder until a regular policy is issued. This applies to fire insurance.

Words Associated with Bookkeeping and Accounting

account	ăc̨ ҽount′	record of debits and credits.
accountant	ăc̨ ҽount′ ănt	one skilled in keeping records.
amount	à mount′	sum total; whole quantity.
auditor	au′ dĭ tõr	one who examines accounts.
balance	băl′ ănc̨e	difference between the two sides of an account.
bookkeeping	bŏŏk′ kēep ĭng	orderly record of transactions.
budget	bŭḋġ′ ĕt	financial statement of needs.
capital	c̨ăp′ ĭ tăl	invested money or property.
creditor	c̨rĕd′ ĭ tõr	one to whom a debt is owed.
debit	dĕb′ ĭt	charge; opposed to credit.
debtor	dĕbt′ õr	one who owes a debt.
depreciation	dĕ prē ci ā′ tion (shĭ)	reduction in value or worth.
earnings	ẽarn′ ĭngs	wages; money earned.
entry	ĕn′ trў	written record of a transaction.
error	ĕr′ rõr	mistake or inaccuracy.
journalizing	joûr′ năl īz ĭng	determining debits and credits.
ledger	lĕḋġ′ ēr	book of final entry.
liabilities	lī à bĭl′ ĭ tĭeş	amount owed; total debts.
posting	pōst′ ĭng	entering sums in a ledger.
proprietorship	prŏ prī′ ĕ tõr shĭp	position of ownership.
receipt	rĕ c̨ēipt′	written acknowledgment.
solvent	sŏl′ vĕnt	able to pay all legal debts.
stockholder	stŏck hōld′ ēr	owner of shares of stock.
system	sўs′ tĕm	plan; orderly arrangement.
transient	trăn′ sient (shĕnt)	momentary; transitory.

Refer to a dictionary for definition, pronunciation, and use of:

acceptance,   erasure,   folio,   footings,   tracer.

Originally the word *budget* referred to a bag or sack with its contents. It has also been used to denote a pouch or wallet of leather, a skin or leather bottle, and a stock or store. It is now used to indicate the financial statement of estimated income and expenditure.

Words Associated with Real Estate

abstract	ăb′ străet	summary of title to land.
bungalow	bŭŋ′ gȧ lō*w*	cottage of a single story.
cistern	çĭs′ tẽrn	reservoir for storing water.
covenants	eȯv′ ĕ nănts	agreements in a deed or lease.
conveyance	eŏn v*e*y′ ănç*e*	deed transferring ownership.
dwelling	dwĕll′ ing	place in which to live.
easement	ēa*s*e′ mĕnt	right to use another's land.
emblements	ĕm′ blĕ mĕnts	annual growing crops.
encumbrance	ĕn eŭm′ brănç*e*	charge or lien upon land.
estate	ĕs tāte′	land or other property.
freehold	frēe′ hōld	life interest in real estate.
grantor	grȧnt′ ŏr	one who makes a conveyance.
improvements	ĭm prọve′ mĕnts	betterments of any kind.
interior	ĭn tē′ rĭ ŏr	inner part, as of a building.
landlord	lănd′ lôrd	owner of land or houses.
lessee	lĕs sēe′	tenant having a lease.
occupancy	ŏe′ eŭ păn çў	act of holding possession.
permanent	pẽr′ mȧ nĕnt	enduring; firmly fixed.
premises	prĕm′ ĭs ĕ*s*	land and its buildings.
quitclaim	quĭt′ clā*i*m	deed relinquishing a right.
realty	rē′ ăl tў	real estate; real property.
restrictions	rĕ strĭe′ tions	limitations; reservations.
section	sĕe′ tion	640 acres of land.
suburban	sŭb ûr′ băn	located in the suburbs.
tenant	tĕn′ ănt	one who leases from another.

Refer to a dictionary for definition, pronunciation, and use of:

dower,   fee simple,   lease,   lessor,   tenement.

The term *landlord* literally means "the lord of the land." A *tenant* means one who holds under another. These words are suggestive of the early English law, the Lord of the Land.

The words *vendee* and *vendor* as legal terms are passing out of common usage.

Stentor was a Grecian whose voice was said to be as loud and powerful as the voices of fifty men together.

Advertising and Printing Terms

advertisement	ăd vẽr′ tĭ*s*e mĕnt	public printed notice.
alphabet	ăl′ phà bĕt	letters used in a language.
announcement	ăn nounçe′ mĕnt	that which is made public.
booklet	bŏok′ lĕt	little book; pamphlet.
caption	eăp′ tion	heading of a chapter; headline.
circular	çĭr′ eŭ lãr	letter for general distribution.
copyright	eŏp′ y̆ rī*ght*	sole right of an author.
editorial	ĕd ĭ tō′ rĭ ăl	article written by an editor.
electrotype	ĕ lĕe′ trŏ tȳpe	plate for use in printing.
emboss	ĕm bŏss′	ornament with raised letter.
engraving	ĕn grāv′ ĭng	print made from a plate.
etching	ĕtch′ ĭng	engraving by use of acids.
illustrator	ĭl′ lŭs trā tŏr	one who draws pictures.
imprint	ĭm prĭnt′	print upon; stamp or mark.
indention	ĭn dĕn′ tion	space at beginning of a line.
information	ĭn fŏr mā′ tion	facts acquired from study.
italic	ĭ tăl′ ĭe	sloping type *like this*.
linotype	lĭn′ ŏ tȳpe	typesetting machine.
lithograph	lĭth′ ŏ grȧph	print reproduced from a stone.
periodical	pē rĭ ŏd′ ĭ eăl	appearing at regular intervals.
placard	plă*e*′ ärd	large printed public notice.
poster	pōst′ ẽr	placard or large bill.
prospectus	prŏ spĕe′ tŭs	circular describing a plan.
publicity	pŭb lĭç′ ĭ tȳ	advertising.
quire	quīr*e*	twenty-four sheets of paper.

Refer to a dictionary for definition, pronunciation, and use of:

capitalize,   comma,   platen,   stereotype,   typography.

A pronunciation test: Determine the correct pronunciation of the following commonly mispronounced words:

abdomen	apparatus	italics	impious	column
penalize	salmon	pumpkin	coupon	mischievous
condolence	suite	veteran	library	literature
comparable	respite	lamentable	senile	laugh

Words Common to Salesmanship

acquaintance	ăe quā*i*nt′ ănçe	person whom one knows.
argument	är′ gû mĕnt	reason; discussion; debate.
attention	ăt tĕn′ tion	faculty of giving heed.
buyer	bu*y*′ ẽr	purchaser.
competitor	eŏm pĕt′ ĭ tŏr	rival.
demonstration	dĕm ȯn strā′ tion	display by way of example.
desirable	dĕ ẓīr′ ȧ bl*e*	worthy of being wanted.
disposal	dĭs pōẓ′ ăl	arrangement; distribution.
dissatisfaction	dĭs săt ĭs făe′ tion	discontent.
distributor	dĭs trĭb′ û tŏr	one who apportions.
jobber	jŏb′ bẽr	one who sells to retailers.
marketable	mär′ kĕt ȧ bl*e*	salable.
material	mȧ tē′ rĭ ăl	having value or importance.
merchantable	mẽr′ chănt ȧ bl*e*	salable; marketable.
misrepresen-	mĭs rĕp rĕ ẓĕn-	false representation.
tation	tā′tion	
novelty	nŏv′ *e*l tў	anything new or different.
personality	pẽr sȯn ăl′ ĭ tў	distinctive individuality.
prospect	prŏs′ pĕet	possible customer.
purchaser	pûr′ chas ẽr (chĭs)	buyer of property.
quibble	quĭb′ bl*e*	evasion; trifling distinction.
seasonable	sēa′ ẓon ȧ bl*e*	suitable to the occasion.
service	sẽrv′ ĭçe	assistance of others.
tact	tăet	ability to handle others.
vanity	văn′ ĭ tў	empty pride; conceit.
wholesale	*w*hōle′ sāl*e*	sell in large quantities.

Refer to a dictionary for definition, pronunciation, and use of:

cater,   economy,   fashion,   huckster,   proposition.

Acadia was the original, and now the poetic name of Nova Scotia.

Academy. *Academeia* was the name of a grove near Athens where the philosopher Plato and his followers met to discuss matters of moment. This is the derivation of our term *academy* as an institution of secondary education. This use of the name is going out of practice.

College is from a Latin word, *collegium*, a society—more particularly a body of persons having a common interest.

Words Common to a City

alderman	ạl′ dẽr mặn	town or city legislator.
alley	ăl′ lĕy̆	narrow passageway.
ambulance	ăm′ bů lănçe	vehicle for carrying the sick.
avenue	ăv′ ĕ nūe	thoroughfare; wide street.
awning	ạwn′ ĭng	rooflike cover.
borough	bor′ ŏugh (bûr)	incorporated town.
boulevard	bọu′ lĕ värd	wide public street.
cabaret	eăb ȧ rẹt′	restaurant with entertainment.
crossing	erŏss′ ĭng	point of intersection.
gutter	gŭt′ tẽr	channel for waste water.
hospital	hŏs′ pĭ tăl	institution for caring for the sick.
hydrant	hȳ′ drănt	street water plug.
mayor	māy′ õr	chief official of a city.
metropolis	mĕ trŏp′ ŏ lĭs	chief or principal city.
metropolitan	mĕt rŏ pŏl′ ĭ tăn	pertaining to a large city.
municipality	mů nĭç ĭ păl′ ĭ ty̆	incorporated town or city.
museum	mů şē′ ŭm	collection of curiosities.
pavement	pāve′ mĕnt	paved street or sidewalk.
policeman	pŏ lïçe′ măn	officer maintaining order.
restaurant	rĕs′ tau rănt (tŏ)	public eating house.
sewerage	sew′ er age (sū′ ẽr ĭj)	system of drainage.
skyscraper	skȳ′ serāp ẽr	very tall building.
theater	thē′ ȧ tẽr	playhouse for dramatic exhibitions.
village	vĭl′ lage (ĭj)	small country hamlet or town.
zoned	zōned	divided into certain districts.

Refer to a dictionary for definition, pronunciation, and use of:

asphalt,   curbstone,   sewage,   suburb,   urban.

An *alderman* is a member of a city governing body. The word is derived from an old English word and refers to a person of rank or dignity second only to that of a king. Time works many changes!

Indiana is known as the "Hoosier State." Why is it so called?

Political and Municipal Terms

alternate	ạl′ tẽr nate (nĭt)	substitute.
anarchist	ăn′ ȧreh ĭst	one opposed to government.
assessor	ăs sĕs′ sõr	one who evaluates property.
cabinet	eăb′ ĭ nĕt	advisory council.
campaign	eăm pāign′	course of action for a cause.
candidate	eăn′ dĭ dāte	office seeker.
census	çĕn′ sŭs	official count of inhabitants.
civilian	çĭ vĭl′ ian (yăn)	one not in the army or navy.
commonwealth	eŏm′ mȯn wĕalth	people of a state; the state.
constitution	eŏn stĭ tū′ tion	organic or fundamental law.
delegate	dĕl′ ĕ gãte	representative.
demagogue	dĕm′ ȧ gŏgue	selfish, political agitator.
inaugurate	ĭn au′ gụ rāte	introduce into office.
national	nă′ tion ăl	relating to a country; country-wide.
nominate	nŏm′ ĭ nāte	name a candidate for office.
nonpartisan	nŏn pär′ tĭ şăn	impartial regarding party interests.
official	ŏf fĭ′ ciăl (fĭsh)	one holding a public office.
opponent	ŏp pō′ nĕnt	foe; adversary; antagonist.
pedestrian	pĕ dĕs′ trĭ ăn	one who travels by foot.
politics	pŏl′ ĭ tĭes	science of government.
primary	prī′ mȧ rў	nominating election.
radical	răd′ ĭ eăl	advocate of extreme measures.
reciprocity	rĕç ĭ prŏç′ ĭ tў	mutual advantages in trade.
republican	rĕ pŭb′ lĭ eăn	member of a political faith.
senator	sĕn′ ȧ tõr	member of a legislative body.

Refer to a dictionary for definition, pronunciation, and use of:

autocratic,   **people,**   **public utilities,**   **tradition.**

A *bribe* is understood to be a price, reward, gift, or inducement given to influence conduct. This word at one time referred to an honest scrap of bread or leavings of a meal that might be given to beggars. Now it commonly applies to a sum of money given to corrupt a person in a position of trust. A dictionary of the year 1660 said: "A peece, lumpe, or cantrill of bread given unto a beggar."

Political and Municipal Terms

ambassador	ăm băs′ sȧ dŏr	government representative.
caucus	¢au′ cŭs	meeting of members of a political party.
citizen	¢ĭt′ ĭ zĕn	civilian; member of a state.
clique	¢lique (klēēk)	exclusive set of persons.
coroner	¢ŏr′ ŏ nēr	one who investigates deaths.
democracy	dĕ mŏe′ rȧ ¢ў̆	"government by the people."
democrat	dĕm′ ŏ ¢răt	advocate of democracy.
dictator	dĭe tā′ tŏr	ruler with unlimited power.
diplomat	dĭp′ lŏ măt	one adept in negotiation.
fusion	fū′ sion (zhŭn)	union of political parties.
government	gŏv′ ērn mĕnt	organized ruling power.
impeachment	ĭm pēach′ mĕnt	accusation of an officer.
inhabitant	ĭn hăb′ ĭt ănt	dweller in a place.
liberty	lĭb′ ēr tў̆	freedom from interference.
lobbying	lŏb′ bў̆ ĭng	influencing a legislator.
monarchy	mŏn′ āre*h* ў̆	government by one ruler.
partisan	pär′ tĭ şăn	devoted adherent to a party.
pension	pĕn′ sion	payment for past services.
platform	plăt′ fôrm	declaration of principles.
population	pŏp û lā′ tion	all the people of a country.
prohibition	prō *h*ĭ bĭ′ tion	act forbidding something.
registration	rĕġ ĭs trā′ tion	enrollment of voters′ names.
suffrage	sŭf′ frag*e* (ĭj)	right to vote; franchise.
township	town′ shĭp	subdivision of a county.
unanimous	û năn′ ĭ moŭs	agreed.

Refer to a dictionary for definition, pronunciation, and use of:

administration, naturalization, representative, socialism, voter.

Buncombe, anything done for mere show or popularity. During the Sixteenth Congress a certain mountaineer congressman from Buncombe county in North Carolina, insisted that he be permitted to "make a speech for Buncombe, as his people expected it," notwithstanding the House was impatient to take a vote on an important matter. From this occurrence we get the slang word for "bunkum" and "bunk."

Political and Municipal Terms

allegiance	ăl lē′ ġĭănçe	fidelity to one's government.
autocracy	au tŏe′ rå çy̆	absolute, uncontrolled power.
ballot	băl′ lŏt	ticket used in voting.
colleague	eŏl′ lēague	one who acts with another.
congress	eŏŋ′ grĕss	national legislative body.
conservative	eŏn sĕrv′ å tĭve	one opposed to change.
convention	eŏn vĕn′ tion	formal political meeting.
council	eoun′ çĭl	legislative body of a city.
despot	dĕs′ pŏt	autocrat; absolute ruler.
electioneer	ĕ lĕe tion ēer′	canvass for political support.
federal	fĕd′ ēr ăl	pertaining to a federation of states.
franchise	frăn′ chīṣe	right to vote.
legislature	lĕġ ĭs lā′ t̬ǔre	law-making body.
liberal	lĭb′ ēr ăl	not bound by authority.
municipal	mŭ nĭç′ ĭ păl	pertaining to a town or city.
nominee	nŏm ĭ nēē′	person named as a candidate.
politician	pŏl ĭ tĭ′ ciăn (tĭsh)	one engaged in party politics.
precinct	prē′ çĭŋet	election district.
prerogative	prĕ rŏg′ å tĭve	exclusive right or privilege.
proxy	prŏx′ y̆	one who acts for another.
quorum	quō′ rŭm	required number of members.
recall	rĕ eall′	act of revoking, as authority.
referendum	rĕf ēr ĕn′ dŭm	right to reject or approve.
sovereign	sŏv′ ēr eĭgn	supreme in authority.
statesman	stātes′ măn	one skilled in public affairs.

Refer to a dictionary for definition, pronunciation, and use of:

constituent, elector, initiative, majority, plurality.

Gerrymander is a term applied to the division of an election district in such a way as to give an unfair advantage to a political party over its opponent. The word was coined when Governor Gerry of Massachusetts caused the state to be divided arbitrarily in an outlandish shape somewhat resembling a salamander; thereby causing a politician to say "better call it a 'gerrymander'."

Writing Vocabulary

autograph	au′ tŏ gráph	person's own signature.
composing	eŏm pōṣ′ ĭng	constructing by mental effort.
copyist	eŏp′ ў ĭst	one who makes transcripts.
crayon	erā*y*′ ŏn	stick of prepared chalk.
engross	ĕn grōss′	write in large letters.
foolscap	fōōlṣ′ eăp	writing paper of a special size.
handwriting	hănd′ *w*rīt ĭng	writing peculiar to a person.
illegible	ĭl lĕǵ′ ĭ bl*e*	unreadable.
inscription	ĭn serĭp′ tion	written characterization.
interline	ĭn tĕr līn*e*′	write between the lines.
legible	lĕǵ′ ĭ bl*e*	plain; readable.
letter	lĕt′ tĕr	written communication.
monogram	mŏn′ ŏ̇ grăm	letters interwoven.
ornamental	ôr nȧ mĕn′ tăl	decorative.
penmanship	pĕn′ măn shĭp	style or manner of handwriting.
records	rĕe′ ŏrdṣ	written or printed reports.
scrawl	serạ*w*l	careless, illegible writing.
scribble	serĭb′ bl*e*	write carelessly.
scribe	serīb*e*	one who copies writing.
script	serĭpt	style of type or letters.
signature	sĭg′ nȧ tụr*e*	person's name written by himself.
spelling	spĕll′ ĭng	naming the letters of a word.
transcript	trăn′ serĭpt	duplicate, written copy.
typist	tȳp′ ĭst	typewriting machine operator.
written	*w*rĭt′ ten	made known in writing.

Refer to a dictionary for definition, pronunciation, and use of:

advantage,   arrange,   invalidate,   loyalty,   sincerely.

Indenture is an agreement in writing between two or more parties wherein each party has a duplicate copy, the parts being separated along a notched edge. The name comes from the practice in early times of indenting or scalloping the instrument on the top side in a waving line. The word is from the Latin, *dentis*, meaning "with the teeth." Hence the literal meaning is to "take a bite out."

Words Pertaining to Correspondence

address	ăd drĕss′	name and direction on a letter.
admissible	ăd mĭs′ sĭ ble	allowable.
clerical	elĕr′ ĭ eăl	relating to office work.
communication	eŏm mū nĭ eā′-tion	oral or written message.
complimentary	eŏm plĭ mĕn′-tá rў	expressive of regard or praise.
correspondence	eŏr rĕ spŏnd′-ĕnçe	communication by letters.
delivery	dĕ lĭv′ ĕrў	transfer of mail.
dictation	dĭe tā′ tion	spoken words to be recorded.
domestic	dŏ mĕs′ tĭe	pertaining to one's country.
envelope	ĕn′ vĕl ōpe	cover for a letter.
heading	hĕad′ ĭng	headline or title.
inclosure	ĭn elō′ sure (zhĕr)	that which is placed within.
manifolding	măn′ ĭ fōld ĭng	making duplicate copies.
message	mĕs′ sage (ĭj)	communication sent.
missive	mĭs′ sĭve	writing containing a message.
postal	pōst′ ăl	relating to the mail service.
postscript	pōst′ serĭpt	addition to a letter.
registered	rĕg′ ĭs tĕred	secure the protection of mail.
salutation	săl û tā′ tion	introductory words of a letter.
secretary	sĕe′ rĕ tar ў (tĕr)	confidential clerk.
stenography	stĕ nŏg′ rá phў	art of writing in shorthand.
superscription	sū pĕr serĭp′ tion	address on an envelope.
typewritten	tўpe′ wrĭt ten	produced on a typewriter.
unmailable	ŭn māĭl′ á ble	not permitted to be mailed.
unsealed	ŭn sēaled′	open for inspection.

Refer to a dictionary for definition, pronunciation, and use of:

devoid,   parcel post,   recommendation,   rural route.

Amanuensis (a tricky word to spell) is from the Latin, *manus*, meaning "by hand." Ordinarily it means a person who is employed to write from dictation or to copy what another has written, as a secretary.

Words Associated with Books

appendix	ăp pĕn' dĭx	something added to a book.
author	au' thŏr	person who writes a book.
chronicles	ehrŏn' ĭ eleş	record of events.
classic	elăs' sĭe	of admitted excellence.
collaboration	eŏl lăb ŏ rā' tion	working together in study.
compilation	eŏm pĭ lā' tion	collection of literary material.
criticism	erĭt' ĭ çĭşm	careful review by a critic.
dictionary	dĭe' tion ar ў (ĕr)	reference book of vocabulary of a language.
figurative	fĭg' ŭr a̍ tĭve	typical and not literal.
gazetteer	găz ĕt tēer'	geographical dictionary.
historical	hĭs tŏr' ĭ eăl	relating to past events.
introduction	ĭn trŏ dŭe' tion	preliminary explanation.
leaflet	lēaf' lĕt	small tract or pamphlet.
library	lĭ' brar ў (brĕr)	collection of books.
literacy	lĭt' ĕr a̍ çў	ability to read and write.
magazine	măg a̍ zïne'	literary periodical.
novelist	nŏv' ĕl ĭst	one who writes fiction.
pictorial	pĭe tō' rĭ ăl	illustrated by pictures.
poem	pō' ĕm	composition written in verse.
publisher	pŭb' lĭsh ĕr	one who issues printed matter.
reminiscence	rĕm ĭ nĭs' çĕnçe	recalling past events.
revision	rĕ vĭ' sion (vĭzh)	act of improving.
royalty	roy' ăl tў	percentage paid to an author.
sequel	sē' quĕl	something that follows.
series	sē' rĭeş	group of items in a succeeding order.

Refer to a dictionary for definition, pronunciation, and use of:

contents,   dialect,   encyclopedia,   excerpt,   whether.

A *book* is a collection of sheets of paper, or other material (blank, written on, or printed), and bound together. The ancient Saxons and Germans used beech boards on which to write by scratching. Hence the word *book* is related to the word *beech* which the early English called *bok*.

John Doe is the fictitious name of a person accused of a crime and whose real name is unknown.

Words Associated with Books

annotation	ăn nŏ tā′ tion	added note or comment.
anonymous	à nŏn′ y̆ moŭs	having unknown authorship.
assemble	ăs sĕm′ ble	collect and fit together.
bibliography	bĭb lĭ ŏg′ rà phy̆	list of descriptive books.
biography	bī ŏg′ rà phy̆	history of a person's life.
chapter	chăp′ tĕr	main division of a book.
commentary	cŏm′ mĕn tar y̆ (tĕr)	book of explanations.
edition	ĕ dĭ′ tion	copies issued at one time.
fiction	fĭe′ tion	imaginary story; novel.
frontispiece	frŏn′ tĭs pĭēçe	illustration facing title page.
hymnal	hy̆m′ năl	book of hymns; hymn book.
illustration	ĭl lŭs trā′ tion	explanatory picture.
literature	lĭt′ ĕr à t̯ůre	notable literary production.
manuscript	măn′ ů serĭpt	author's original copy.
pamphlet	păm′ phlĕt	small unbound book.
plagiarist	plā′ ḡĭ à rĭst	literary thief.
preamble	prē′ ăm ble	introductory statement.
preface	prĕf′ ace (ĭs)	introductory explanation.
publications	pŭb lĭ eā′ tionş	books offered for sale.
romance	rŏ mănçe′	story based upon idealism.
supplement	sŭp′ plĕ mĕnt	addition to a publication.
typographical	ty̆ pŏ grăph′ ĭ eăl	pertaining to printing.
vellum	vĕl′ lŭm	fine parchment usually made from calfskin.
vocabulary	vŏ eăb′ů lar y̆ (lĕr)	words used by a person.
volume	vŏl′ ůme	single book.

Refer to a dictionary for definition, pronunciation, and use of:

autobiography,   glossary,   memoirs,   narrative,   translation.

We may live without poetry, music and art;
We may live without conscience, and live without heart;
We may live without friends; we may live without books;
But civilized man cannot live without cooks.

—OWEN MEREDITH.

Words Associated with Education

biology	bī ŏl′ ō ġȳ	science of living things.
botany	bŏt′ à nȳ	science of plant life.
calisthenics	eăl ĭs thĕn′ ĭes	light gymnastic exercises.
curriculum	eŭr rĭe′ ū lŭm	organized courses of study.
discipline	dĭs′ cĭ plĭne	training of mind or manners.
edification	ĕd ĭ fĭ eā′ tion	enlightenment; instruction.
education	ĕd ū eā′ tion	schooling.
faculty	făe′ ŭl tȳ	body of teachers or professors.
ignoramus	ĭg nŏ rā′ mŭs	dunce; ignorant person.
illiterate	ĭl lĭt′ ĕr ate (ĭt)	uneducated or ignorant person.
instill	ĭn stĭll′	inculcate; infuse; impart.
instruction	ĭn strŭe′ tion	knowledge given or imparted.
laboratory	lăb′ ō rå tō rȳ	room used for experiments.
matriculate	må trĭe′ ū lāte	enroll in a college or university.
novice	nŏv′ ĭçe	beginner; tyro; learner.
paraphrase	păr′ à phrāşe	restatement of an expression.
pedagogy	pĕd à gō′ ġȳ	principles and methods of teaching.
persuasion	pĕr suā′ sion (zhŭn)	act of influencing the mind.
principal	prĭn′ çĭ pal	official in a school.
professor	prŏ fĕs′ sŏr	teacher of a specialty.
science	scī′ ĕnçe	body of organized knowledge.
semester	sĕ mĕs′ tĕr	scholastic half-year.
studious	stū′ dĭ oŭs	diligent in study.
tuition	tū ĭ′ tion	price paid for instruction.
university	ū nĭ vẽr′ sĭ tȳ	related group of colleges.

Refer to a dictionary for definition, pronunciation, and use of:

correlation,   **discourse,**   **enlighten,**   **logic,**   **tutor.**

Educate means "to train and cultivate the mental, the moral, and the physical well-being of an individual." It is derived from the Latin, *educare,* "to lead," or "to bring or draw forth." Literally it means "to train a child in the way it should go so that it will not depart therefrom."

Words are the wings of action.

—LAVATER.

Words Associated with Education

achievement	à chĭēve′ měnt	accomplishment.
diploma	dĭ plō′ mà	certificate of graduation.
disseminate	dĭs sěm′ ĭ nāte	spread a truth or opinion.
docile	dŏç′ ĭle	easily taught or managed.
emulate	ěm′ ů lāte	try to equal or excel.
environment	ěn vī′ ròn měnt	surrounding influence.
examination	ěx̱ ăm ĭ nā′ tion	test.
fallacy	făl′ là çў	false idea or notion.
freshman	frěsh′ măn	first-year student.
graduate	grăd′ů āte	complete a prescribed course.
ignorance	ĭg′ nŏ rănçe	lack of knowledge.
inculcate	ĭn ᴇŭl′ ᴇāte	impress upon the mind.
intelligence	ĭn těl′ lĭ ǧěnçe	power of understanding.
lecture	lĕe′ t̲u̲re	formal instructive address.
memorize	měm′ŏ rīze	learn by heart.
philosophy	phĭ lŏs′ ŏ phў	"love of knowledge."
preceptor	prĕ çĕp′ tŏr	instructor or teacher.
punctuality	pŭŋe t̲u̲ ăl′ ĭ tў	promptness.
recitation	rěç ĭ tā′ tion	act of repeating a lesson.
repetition	rěp ē tĭ′ tion	reiteration.
rudiment	r̲u̲′ dĭ měnt	beginning of any knowledge.
scholastic	seℎŏ lăs′ tĭe	pertaining to scholarship.
sorority	sŏ rŏr′ ĭ tў	girls' or women's society.
teachable	tēaℎ′ à ble	able or willing to learn.
visual	vis′ ů ăl (vĭzh)	conveying a mental vision.

Refer to a dictionary for definition, pronunciation, and use of:

alma mater,   analytical,   civics,   dean,   monograph.

Pedagogue literally means "a boy-leader." The word now designates a teacher of children or a "schoolmaster." The word has come down to us from Classical antiquity and refers to a slave whose duty it was to attend his master's sons in their youth and to accompany them to and from school. In time the attendant became the tutor of the children, and eventually the teacher in the classroom. A schoolmaster is still presumed to "lead" his charges, morally and otherwise.

Words Common in the Study of English

abbreviation	ăb brē vĭ ā′ tion	shortened, contracted form.
accent	ăe′ çĕnt	emphasis; stress of voice.
adverb	ăd′ vẽrb	word that modifies a verb, adjective, or adverb.
antecedent	ăn tĕ çēd′ ĕnt	that for which a pronoun stands.
apostrophe	à pŏs′ trŏ phĕ	mark indicating an omission.
attribute	ăt′ trĭ būte	essential characteristic.
climax	elī′ măx	highest point; culmination.
complement	eŏm′ plĕ mĕnt	something that completes.
definition	dĕf ĭ nĭ′ tion	description or explanation.
diphthong	dĭph′ thŏng	two vowels sounded as one.
doggerel	dŏg′ gẽr ĕl	absurd, irregular verse.
eloquence	ĕl′ ŏ quĕnçe	lofty and fluent discourse.
etymology	ĕt ў̆ mŏl′ ŏ ġў̆	origin and science of words.
exclamatory	ĕx elăm′ à tō rў̆	expressing strong emotions.
grammar	grăm′ mãr	science of a language.
hackneyed	hăck′ neў̆ed	much used; commonplace.
imperative	ĭm pĕr′ à tĭve	expressing positive command.
interjection	ĭn tẽr jĕc′ tion	word expressing emotion.
masculine	măs′ eũ lĭne	denoting the male sex.
paragraph	păr′ à gràph	subdivision of a composition.
pronoun	prō′ noun	word used instead of a noun.
pronunciation	prŏ nŭn çĭ ā′ tion	manner of speaking words.
quotation	quŏ tā′ tion	words credited to another.
rhetoric	rhĕt′ ŏ rĭe	expressive language; oratory.
syntax	sў̆n′ tăx	construction of sentences.

Refer to a dictionary for definition, pronunciation, and use of:

collective,   college,   English,   nominative,   preposition.

Dunce, a dull-witted person, or one backward in book learning. The word is taken from *Duns Scotus*, a learned schoolmaster of the thirteenth century who was given to "splitting hairs" over trivial matters. His followers were called "Dunsers" as an expression of contempt for their sophistry.

Words Common in the Study of English

alliteration	ăl lĭt ẽr ā′ tion	repetition of similar sounds.
aptitude	ăp′ tĭ tūde	capacity for learning; talent.
comparison	ϲŏm păr′ ĭ sȯn	modification denoting degree.
composition	ϲŏm pȯ ṣĭ′ tion	literary production; essay.
culture	ϲŭl′ tу̦re	refinement of manners.
derivative	dĕ rĭv′ à tĭve	taken from another; secondary.
diffuseness	dĭf fūse′ nĕss	state of being "wordy."
epithet	ĕp′ ĭ thĕt	descriptive adjective.
hyphen	hȳ′ phĕn	connecting mark, thus -.
idiom	ĭd′ ĭ ȯm	peculiarity of a language.
neuter	neū′ tẽr	neither masculine nor feminine.
normal	nôr′ măl	average; regular.
objective	ŏb jĕe′ tĭve	case, not nominative or possessive.
phraseology	phrā ṣĕ ŏl′ ȯ ġy̆	manner of expression; style.
positive	pŏṣ′ ĭ tĭve	simple form of an adjective.
possessive	pŏs ṣĕs′ sĭve	case indicating ownership.
primitive	prĭm′ ĭ tĭve	first in time; primary.
redundancy	rĕ dŭn′ dăn çy̆	use of unnecessary words.
sentence	sĕn′ tĕnçe	thought expressed in words.
superlative	sŭ pẽr′ là tĭve	highest or lowest degree.
terseness	tẽrse′ nĕss	brief comprehensiveness.
theme	thēme	short composition.
trite	trīte	stale; worn out; commonplace.
verbiage	vẽr′ bĭ age (ĭj)	unnecessary use of words.
vernacular	vẽr năe′ ů lãr	language of a locality.

Refer to a dictionary for definition, pronunciation, and use of:

complex,   enunciate,   lucid,   oration,   voice.

Plurality and *majority* are often confused. If a contestant for an office receives more votes than any other candidate, he is said to have received a *plurality*. If the contestant receives more votes than all the other candidates combined, he is said to have received a *majority*. If A receives fifty votes, B thirty votes, and C twenty votes, A has a plurality, but not a majority. If there are only two candidates, the *plurality* and *majority* are the same.

1/7/44

LESSON 34

Words Common in the Study of English

adjective	ăd′ jĕe tĭve	qualifying noun or pronoun.
articulation	är tĭe ũ lā′ tion	act of speaking distinctly.
condense	eŏn dĕnse′	render more compact.
conjunction	eŏn jŭŋe′ tion	word used to join other words.
construction	eŏn strŭe′ tion	arrangement of words.
diacritical	dī à erĭt′ ĭ eăl	pertaining to marks indicating sounds.
diagraming	dī′ à grăm ĭng	explaining graphically.
diction	dĭe′ tion	manner of speaking.
epigram	ĕp′ ĭ grăm	concise, pithy saying.
feminine	fĕm′ ĭ nĭne	pertaining to a woman.
gender	ġĕn′ dẽr	distinction of sex in words.
interrogative	ĭn tẽr rŏġ′ à tĭve	word indicating a question.
language	lăŋ′ guaġe (gwĭj)	means of expressing thought.
negative	nĕg′ à tĭve	word expressing denial.
obsolete	ŏb′ sŏ lēte	antiquated or out of use.
orthography	ôr thŏg′ rà phў	art of correct spelling.
parsing	pärs′ ĭng	classifying grammatically.
plural	plṳ′ răl	expressing more than one.
punctuation	pŭŋe tṳ ā′ tion	art of using marks or stops.
simile	sĭm′ ĭ lē	certain figure of speech.
singular	sĭŋ′ gṳ lär	denoting one person or thing.
subject	sŭb′ jĕet	basic theme of an essay.
subordinate	sŭb ôr′ dĭnate (nĭt)	"unable to stand alone."
synopsis	sỹn ŏp′ sĭs	abstract or summary.
treatise	trēa′ tĭse	long and formal composition.

Refer to a dictionary for definition, pronunciation, and use of:

abridge,   paradox,   prefix,   suffix,   title.

Philosophy. This word literally means a "love of wisdom." It is derived from a Greek word. It is said to have been suggested by Socrates who chose to call himself "a lover of wisdom." It is said that upon being complimented on his wisdom, he said he was not wise but a lover of wisdom, the Deity alone being wise.

What is the difference between *no admittance* and *no admission?*

44

LESSON 35

Pertaining to Farming

acreage	ā′ ere age (kēr ĭj)	acres in a tract of land.
agriculture	ăg′ rĭ eŭl t̤ure	art of cultivating the ground.
arable	ăr′ à ble	fit for cultivation.
cultivate	eŭl′ tĭ vāte	improve growth by tillage.
cultivator	eŭl′ tĭ vā tŏr	farm tool for removing weeds.
ensilage	ĕn′ sĭ lage (lĭj)	preserved green fodder.
erosion	ĕ rō′ sion (zhŭn)	wearing away of the soil.
fallow	făl′ lōw	land uncultivated for a season.
fertilizer	fĕr′ tĭ līz ēr	that which enriches the soil.
fodder	fŏd′ dēr	dry coarse food for cattle.
forage	fŏr′ age (ĭj)	food for horses and cattle.
granary	grăn′ à rẙ	storehouse for grain.
harness	här′ nĕss	equipment for a horse.
harvest	här′ vĕst	gathering ripened crops.
heifer	hĕĭf′ ēr	full-grown young cow.
horticulture	hôr′ tĭ eŭl t̤ure	cultivating gardens, orchards.
humus	hū′ mŭs	decayed vegetable matter.
irrigation	ĭr rĭ gā′ tion	watering land artificially.
meadow	mĕad′ ōw	low level grass land.
mower	mōw′ ēr	machine for cutting grass.
orchard	ôr′ chärd	inclosure of fruit trees.
pasture	pȧs′ t̤ure	field for grazing animals.
reaper	rēap′ ēr	machine for cutting grain.
thresher	thrĕsh′ ēr	threshing machine.
tillable	tĭll′ à ble	arable; fit for the plow.

Refer to a dictionary for definition, pronunciation, and use of:

fruitful,   harrow,   mulch,   silo,   vegetable.

Spelling is chiefly a habit of the eye, and is of practical use only in writing. The student should therefore be trained to see word forms correctly.

—REED.

It is no great merit to spell well, but it is a great demerit to spell ill.
—From an old spelling book.

LESSON 36	LESSON 37	LESSON 38
Farm Terms	Fruits	Vegetables
alfalfa	apples	artichoke
barley	apricots	asparagus
buckwheat	bananas	beans
cantaloupes	blackberry	broccoli
cattle	cherry	cabbage
clover	coconut	carrots
cotton	cranberry	cauliflower
dairying	date	celery
fowls	gooseberry	chicory
fruits	grapefruit	cucumber
grain	huckleberry	dandelion
Kafir corn	lemon	lettuce
maize	loganberry	okra
melons	mulberry	onions
millet	olive	parsley
potatoes	orange	parsnips
poultry	peach	peppers
pumpkins	pear	potatoes
rutabaga	persimmon	radish
sorghum	pineapple	rhubarb
sugar cane	plum	salsify
timothy	prune	spinach
tobacco	quince	squash
turkeys	raspberry	tomato
wheat	strawberry	turnip

If a corporation issues stock for insufficient value or for no consideration at all, the stock is said to be *watered*. The value of such shares of stock in the hands of a stockholder is diluted to the extent that the stock is issued without adequate payment having been made for it. The holders of watered stock are liable to subsequent creditors who are unaware of the facts.

The issuance of watered stock is held to be a fraud against creditors and such practice is prohibited by law. Stocks may be watered in several ways.

The term *watered stock* is said to have originated when the owner of a herd of beef cattle sold his herd to a neighbor, and before the sale he fed the cattle salt and then watered them heavily. This increased their weight but their value, of course, was unchanged.

mor 1/09/44

Trees and Lumber Terms

basswood	băss' wŏŏd	whitewood (also called "bass").
boards	bōardş	thin, flat pieces of timber.
catalpa	ċȧ tăl' på	ornamental flowering tree.
cedar	çē' dår	fragrant evergreen tree.
chestnut	chĕs*t'* nŭt	wood or fruit of a chestnut tree.
cypress	çȳ' prĕss	large cone-bearing tree.
ebony	ĕb' ȯn y̆	hard, heavy, black wood.
foliage	fō' lĭ ag*e* (ĭj)	leaves of a plant or tree.
hemlock	hĕm' lŏck	bark useful for tanning leather.
hickory	hĭck' ȯ ry̆	hardwood, nut-bearing tree.
kiln-dried	kĭl*n*'-drīe*d*	dried in an oven.
knot	*k*nŏt	gnarled part of a tree.
locust	lō' ċŭst	tree having durable wood.
logging	lŏg' gĭng	felling and hauling trees.
mahogany	må hŏg' å ny̆	valuable tropical tree.
maple	mā' pl*e*	light-colored, very firm wood.
pecan	pĕ ċăn'	species of hickory tree.
picket	pĭck' ĕt	fence paling; pointed stick.
poplar	pŏp' lår	tree of very rapid growth.
quartered	quạr' tēre*d*	sawed lumber to show the grain.
slab	slăb	outer cut sawed from a log.
surfaced	sûr' faced (fĭst)	lumber dressed by a planer.
sycamore	sy̆e' å mōr*e*	useful shade tree.
walnut	wạl' nŭt	tree valuable for lumber.
willow	wĭl' lō*w*	tree with slender branches.

Refer to a dictionary for definition, pronunciation, and use of:

birch,   forestry,   holly,   leaves,   spruce.

Lumber, timber sawed or split into boards, beams, or planks of small dimension ready for use. The word originally meant "useless furniture." At one time it signified a pawnbroker's shop or storeroom. The word is derived from *Lombard*, an early banker whose rooms were said to be crowded with articles received as pledges for loans.

Some books are to be tested; others swallowed; and some few to be chewed and digested.

— Bacon.

47

Pertaining to Cookery

biscuit	bĭs′ ҽuĭt	small cake or loaf of bread.
boiling	boil′ ĭng	bubbling up with heat.
bouillon	bouillon′(bōō yôN′)	thin, clear soup or broth.
canning	ҽăn′ nĭng	method of preserving foods in tins or cans.
chowder	chow′ dĕr	soup made of fish or clams.
consomme	ҽôn sŏm mҽ′	strong, clear broth of meat.
culinary	ҽū′ lĭ nar y̆ (nẽr)	pertaining to cookery.
delicious	dĕ lĭ′ cious (lĭsh ŭs)	very pleasing to the taste.
dietary	dī′ ĕ tar y̆ (tĕr)	pertaining to rules of diet.
entree	en′ tree (än′ trā)	subordinate, or side-dish.
flavoring	flā′ võr ĭng	extract used for seasoning.
fricassee	frĭe ȧs sēē′	cooked meat, stewed in gravy.
garbage	gär′ bage (ĭj)	kitchen waste or refuse.
giblets	ġĭb′ lĕts	internal organs of poultry.
mayonnaise	māy ŏn nāiṣe′	thick sauce or salad dressing.
menu	mĕn′ ū	list of foods to be served.
meringue	mẽ ringue′ (răng′)	icing of sugar and eggs.
muffins	mŭf′ fĭnṣ	small, light, round cakes.
nutritious	nŭ trĭ′ tious (trĭsh ŭs)	nourishing.
omelet	ŏm′ ĕ lĕt	dish consisting mainly of eggs.
puree	pŭ rҽe′	thickened soup.
relish	rĕl′ ĭsh	pleasing appetizing flavor.
simmer	sĭm′ mẽr	boil slowly and gently.
succotash	sŭҽ′ ҽð tăsh	cooked fresh corn and beans.
waffles	wạf′ fleṣ	indented battercakes.

Refer to a dictionary for definition, pronunciation, and use of:

albumen,   brisket,   casein,   coddled,   scrambled.

The word *omelet*, meaning "a dish of fried eggs beaten up with flour and milk and cooked in a frying pan." Often chopped ham, parsley, cheese or other ingredients are added to give special tang. The word is derived from the Latin, *lamella*, literally meaning "a thin piece of metal." The name of this dish indicates its shape or form rather than the material from which it is made.

Wed.

Pertaining to Nutriment

banquet	băŋ′ quĕt	rich or costly feast.
beverage	bĕv′ ēr ag*e* (ĭj)	liquid for drinking.
cafeteria	eăf ĕ tēr′ ĭ à	self-serving restaurant.
calorie	eăl′ ŏ rĭ*e*	unit of energy value of food.
condiment	eŏn′ dĭ mĕnt	seasoning for food; relish.
confectionery	eŏn fĕe′ tion ĕr ў	candy and pastry collectively.
delicacy	dĕl′ ĭ eà çў	food pleasing to the taste.
dessert	deş şērt′ (dĭ)	sweets served after dinner.
digestible	dĭ ġĕst′ ĭ bl*e*	capable of being assimilated.
edible	ĕd′ ĭ bl*e*	fit or safe for eating.
gluttony	glŭt′ ton ў	excess or overeating.
jellies	jĕl′ lĭeş	foods made from fruit juices.
luncheon	lŭnch′ eŏn	light meal about midday.
mastication	măs tĭ eā′ tion	act of chewing food.
nibble	nĭb′ bl*e*	bite in small bits.
palatable	păl′ at à ble (ĭt)	agreeable to the taste.
pastry	pās′ trў	pies, tarts, and similar foods.
protein	prō′ tĕ ĭn	tissue-building substance.
provisions	prŏ vĭ′ sions (vĭzh)	stock or supply of foods.
ration	rā′ tion	fixed allowance of food.
ravenous	răv′ ĕn oŭs	extremely hungry; greedy.
repast	rĕ pàst′	food taken at a meal.
salad	săl′ ăd	chopped fruits or vegetables.
sustenance	sŭs′ tĕ nănç*e*	that which supports life.
viands	vī′ ăndş	articles of food; provisions.

Refer to a dictionary for definition, pronunciation, and use of:

savory,   snack,   spices,   subsistence,   sweetmeats.

Graham bread and flour are named after Sylvester Graham, a physician and vegetarian, who lived in the early part of the last century. Graham flour is the finely ground meal of the whole grain of wheat. Dr. Graham was an advocate of the use of unbolted wheat flour which now bears his name and is used very extensively.

Meridian literally pertains to the midday, but figuratively it is the highest or culminating point of anything. Geographically it has reference to the great circle passing through the poles north and south.

Provisions

catchup *or*	eătch′ ŭp	sauce made from tomatoes
catsup	eăt′ sŭp	and used for flavoring.
cayenne	eay ĕnne′ (kī)	hot, pungent red pepper.
cheese	chēēṣe	curd of milk, used as food.
chocolate	chŏe′ ŏ late (lĭt)	preparation from cacao seed.
cinnamon	çĭn′ nȧ mȯn	aromatic bark of a tree.
citron	çĭt′ rȯn	fruit resembling a lemon.
coffee	eôf′ fēē	roasted seed used for a drink.
eatable	ēat′ ȧ ble	good or fit to be eaten.
gelatin	ġĕl′ ȧ tĭn	animal food substance.
halibut	hăl′ ĭ bŭt	large flat food fish.
hominy	hŏm′ ĭ nỹ	hulled and ground corn.
lobster	lŏb′ stēr	large marine shellfish.
luscious	lŭṣ′ cioŭs (lŭsh)	pleasing to the taste.
macaroni	măe ȧ rō′ nĭ	dried tube of wheat paste.
mutton	mŭt′ ton	flesh of sheep used for food.
oleomargarine	ō lĕ ŏ mär′ ġȧ rïne	substitute for butter.
oysters	oys′ tērṣ	soft shellfish used for food.
pickles	pĭck′ leṣ	food preserved in brine.
salmon	sălm′ ȯn	large, yellowish red fish.
sandwich	sănd′ wĭch	slices of bread inclosing food.
sardine	sär dïne′	small fish preserved in oil.
sirloin	sïr′ loin	choice cut of beef.
tapioca	tăp ĭ ō′ eȧ	food from the cassava root.
vanilla	vȧ nĭl′ lȧ	pungent flavoring extract.
vinegar	vĭn′ ĕ gär	sour liquid relish.

Refer to a dictionary for definition, pronunciation, and use of:

almond, bologna, sirup, spaghetti, syrup.

The word *catsup*, also written *catchup* and *ketchup*, is derived from a Malay word spelled *kechap*, and means "a spice or condiment." Generally speaking, *catsup* is a spiced condiment for meats. It is usually made from the juice of mushrooms, walnuts, tomatoes, and the like. A tomato sauce or catsup is made from tomatoes seasoned with vinegar, spice, and sugar.

Provisions

mon.
1/24/44

allspice	ạll′ spīçe	mild, pungent condiment.
bacon	bā′ ėon	side of hog meat, salted.
butter	bŭt′ tẽr	fat obtained from cream.
cloves	ᴄlōveṣ	pungent aromatic spice.
cocoa	ᴄō′ ᴄōa	chocolate, deficient in fat.
crackers	ᴄrăck′ ẽrṣ	dry, thin, crisp biscuits.
delicatessen	dĕl ĭ ᴄȧ tĕs′ sĕn	prepared foods for sale.
ginger	ġĭn′ ġẽr	pungent aromatic rootstock.
glucose	glụ′ ᴄōse	sirup made from corn starch.
gravy	grā′ vў	juice of cooked meat.
herring	hĕr′ rĭng	small, ocean food fish.
honey	hȯn′ ў (hŭn)	sweet fluid collected by bees.
lemonade	lĕm ȯn āde′ (ŭn)	drink made of lemon juice.
lentils	lĕn′ tĭlṣ	flat, lens-shaped pea seed.
mackerel	măck′ ẽr ĕl	food sea fish.
molasses	mȯ lăs′ sĕṣ	sirup made from sugar or sap.
nutmeg	nŭt′ mĕg	seed used as a condiment.
pheasant	phĕaṣ′ ănt	gaily colored wild fowl.
preserves	prĕ ṣẽrveṣ′	fruit cooked in a sirup.
raisins	rāỉ′ ṣĭnṣ	species of dried grape.
sauerkraut	sauer′ kraut (sour′ krout)	cut and fermented cabbage.
sausage	sau′ sage (sĭj)	seasoned, ground fresh pork.
sherbet	shẽr′ bĕt	drink made of fruit juice.
squab	squạb	young hatched pigeon.
sugar	sụg′ ãr	sweet vegetable substance.

Refer to a dictionary for definition, pronunciation, and use of:

caviar,   creamery,   pasteurize,   sage,   victuals.

Grocer, a dealer in tea, coffee, sugar, dried fruits, and provisions. The word should be distinguished from *grosser*, meaning "larger, coarser, or ruder." Both words are derived from the same source and originally referred to one who sells by the gross, or wholesale. This word has now reversed itself.

It should be noted that *grocery* and *corner grocery* are often designated as a drinking-place.

Pertaining to the Household

bedstead	bĕd′ stĕad	frame support for a bed.
bolster	bōl′ stẽr	long pillow or cushion.
buffet	bụf fẹt′	sideboard or cupboard.
chandelier	çhăn dĕ li͝ẽr′	hanging fixture for lights.
cooker	co͝ok′ ẽr	special cooking apparatus.
cupboard	cŭp′ bŏard	cabinet for dishes or food.
curtain	cûr′ taĭn	ornamental hanging drapery.
decorations	dĕe ŏ rā′ tiọns	that which adorns or beautifies.
draperies	drā′ pẽr ĭẹs	fabrics used for curtains.
furnace	fûr′ nace (nĭs)	apparatus for producing heat.
hamper	hăm′ pẽr	large covered basket.
hostess	hōst′ ĕss	woman who entertains guests.
mission	mĭs′ sion	peculiar style of furniture.
pillow	pĭl′ lō*w*	sack filled with feathers.
portiere	pōr tiere′ (tyâr′)	curtain hanging at a doorway.
queen's ware	que͞en′ş wâr*e*	cream-colored earthenware.
radio	rā′ dĭ ō	communication by means of waves.
refrigerator	rẽ frĭg′ ẽr ā tŏr	box for keeping food cool.
rocker	rŏck′ ẽr	chair set on rockers.
serviceable	sẽrv′ ĭçe à ble	durable; useful and lasting.
settee	sĕt tē͞e′	long seat with a back.
towel	tow′ ĕl	washing or drying cloth.
upholster	ŭp hōl′ stẽr	provide with textile coverings.
wardrobe	wạrd′ rōb*e*	portable closet for clothes.
window	wĭn′ dō*w*	opening to admit light.

Refer to a dictionary for definition, pronunciation, and use of:

carpet,   colonial,   dinette,   pedestal,   velours.

The word *alphabet* is of interesting origin. It is formed from a combination of two Greek letters, *alpha* and *beta*, the first and second letters in the Greek alphabet. It will thus be noted that this word is compounded from letters only corresponding to our A and B. That makes it as simple as A B C.

Pertaining to the Household

Axminster	Ăx' mĭn stẽr	imitation Turkish carpet.
bedding	bĕd' dĭng	bed covering or clothes.
broiler	broil' ẽr	utensil for broiling.
bureau	bū' reau (rō)	chest of drawers; a dresser.
chiffonier	çhĭf fŏ nïer'	high chest of drawers.
closet	clŏṣ' ĕt	small room or apartment.
coverlet	ĕov' ẽr lĕt	ornamental bedspread.
crockery	crŏck' ẽr y̌	earthenware vessels.
davenport	dăv' ĕn pōrt	long, low, upholstered sofa.
dishes	dĭsh' ĕs	vessels for serving food.
divan	dĭ' văn	low cushioned couch.
dresser	drĕss' ẽr	bureau, with a mirror.
furniture	fûr' nĭ t̤u̧re	movable household goods.
hassock	hăs' sȯck	stuffed cushion; footstool.
jardiniere	jär dĭ nïere'	ornamental vase for plants.
kitchen	kĭtch' ĕn	room set apart for cookery.
linoleum	lĭ nō' lė ŭm	composition floor covering.
mattress	măt' trĕss	tick stuffed and tufted.
mirror	mĭr' rŏr	looking-glass; reflector.
parlor	pär' lŏr	room for receiving guests.
piano	pĭ ăn' ō	stringed musical instrument.
porcelain	pōr' çĕ laĭn	translucent earthenware.
radiator	rā' dĭ ā tōr	device for diffusing heat.
sofa	sō' fȧ	long, upholstered couch.
tapestry	tăp' ĕs try̌	fabric used for wall hangings.

Refer to a dictionary for definition, pronunciation, and use of:

commode,   couch,   lounge,   moquette,   ottoman.

Linoleum is derived from the combination of the Latin *linum,* meaning
"flax," and *oleum,* meaning "oil." *Linseed oil* is a product of flaxseed.
The word was coined by Frederick Walton to describe this type of a
floor covering. Walton found that linseed oil mixed with gum and pressed
into a backing of burlap provided an excellent binder when the oil oxidized.

The literal meaning of *ledger* is "a book that lies on a desk."

Pertaining to Clothing

blouse	blouᶊe	loose outer garment.
bonnet	bŏn′ nĕt	covering for the head.
burlap	bûr′ lăp	coarse fabric made of hemp.
costume	cŏs′ tūme	dress in general; clothes.
cravenette	erā vĕn ĕtte′	woolen waterproof raincoat.
embroidery	ĕm broi′ dĕr y̆	ornamental needlework.
fascinator	făs′ çĭ nā tŏr	knit head covering.
fashionable	făsh′ ᵢŏn à ble	conforming to current style.
hosiery	hō′ sier y̆ (zhĕr)	stockings or socks.
jacket	jăck′ ĕt	short tailless coat.
laundry	laun′ dry̆ (lôn)	place where clothes are washed.
lingerie	lin ge rie′ (län′ zhĕ rē)	undergarments for women.
mercerized	mĕr′ çĕr īzed	made to resemble silk.
millinery	mĭl′ lĭ nĕr y̆	women's hats or bonnets.
mitten	mĭt′ ten	covering for the hand.
oxford	ŏx′ fŏrd	low, laced shoe.
remnant	rĕm′ nănt	that which remains; scrap.
ruching	ru̧ch′ ĭng	decorative edging.
seersucker	sēer′ su̧ek ēr	crinkled cotton fabric.
shoddy	shŏd′ dy̆	cloth of an inferior quality.
smock	smŏck	long, loose outer garment.
tailor	tāᵢ′ lŏr	one who makes garments.
trousers	trou′ ᶊĕrᶊ	garment worn by men or boys.
woolen	wŏŏl′ ĕn	any cloth made from wool.
worsted	wo̧r′ stĕd	British expression for woolen.

Refer to a dictionary for definition, pronunciation, and use of:

attire, gaberdine, negligee, toilet, washable.

Advertise, "give public notice." French, *avertir;* from the Latin, *adver-tere*, "to turn to." The thought is that of turning public attention to the thing advertised. The word *advertise* was formerly accented on the second syllable, later on the last syllable, and now the accent is on the first syllable.

Remember that the word *English* always begins with a capital *E.* Do the names of all other languages begin with capitals?

Frid.

Pertaining to Clothing

apparel	ăp păr′ ĕl	clothing for the body.
apron	ā′ prŏn	garment protecting clothes.
corduroy	ĉôr′ dŭ roy	heavy, thick-ribbed cloth.
cuffs	ĉŭffs	wrist part of sleeves.
gabardine	găb ăr dïne′	fabric resembling serge.
garment	gär′ mĕnt	any article of clothing.
gauntlet	gaunt′ lĕt (gônt)	glove with wrist extension.
handkerchief	hăŋd′ kĕr chĭef	cloth for wiping the face.
khaki	khä′ kï	cloth of a brownish color.
kimono	kĭ mō′ nō	loose, outer dressing gown.
mackintosh	măck′ ĭn tŏsh	waterproof outer garment.
necktie	nĕck′ tïe	tie worn under the chin.
overalls	ō′ vĕr ạlls̱	protective over-trousers.
pajamas	på jä′ mås̱	loose, sleeping garment.
seamstress	sēam′ strĕss	dressmaker or needlewoman.
skirt	skïrt	lower and hanging part of a dress.
sleeve	slēēve	part of a garment covering the arm.
slippers	slĭp′ pĕrs̱	light, low, loose shoes.
suspenders	sŭs pĕnd′ ĕrs̱	braces to hold up trousers.
sweater	swĕat′ ĕr	thick woolen jacket or jersey.
texture	tĕx′ tu̱re	construction of a fabric.
ulster	ŭl′ stĕr	long, loose overcoat.
underwear	ŭn′ dĕr weâr	underclothes.
uniform	ū′ nĭ fôrm	distinctive dress of an order.
waistcoat	wāist′ ĉōat	man's sleeveless garment.

Refer to a dictionary for definition, pronunciation, and use of:

finery,   garb,   leggings,   raiment,   stockings.

Apparel, refers in a general way to dress, garments, clothing, or attire. In former times it referred to an ornamental dress, "to cover with something ornamental." This is probably what Shakespeare had in mind when he said: "The apparel oft proclaims the man." The word is derived from the Latin *ad* and *par*, meaning "to make equal or similar."

Pertaining to Dry Goods

bobbinet	bŏb bĭ nĕt′	machine-made lace.
brilliantine	brĭl lian tĭne′ (yăn)	dress fabric like alpaca.
brocade	brŏ ᴄāde′	silk fabric with raised figure.
cashmere	ᴄăsh′ mēre	soft, woolen dress goods.
cassimere	ᴄăs′ sĭ mēre	thin, twilled woolen cloth.
challis	çhăl′ lĭs	light-weight woolen fabric.
chambray	çhăm′ brăy	gingham with linen finish.
cheviot	çhĕv′ ĭ ŏt	rough twilled woolen cloth.
chiffon	çhĭf′ fŏn	soft, thin, gauzy material.
crinoline	ᴄrĭn′ ŏ lĭne	stiff fabric used for lining.
denim	dĕn′ ĭm	cloth used for making overalls.
dimity	dĭm′ ĭ tў	fabric with raised stripes.
gingham	gĭng′ hăm	cloth with a stripe or check.
hemstitch	hĕm′ stĭtch	ornamental needlework.
madras	mȧ drȧs′	corded or figured fabric.
organdie	ôr′ găn dĭe	light transparent muslin.
percale	pēr ᴄāle′	smoothly finished cotton cloth.
sateen	sȧ tēen′	fabric resembling satin.
sheeting	shēet′ ĭng	material for making bed sheets.
silkaline	sĭlk ȧ lĭne′	soft, thin mercerized cloth.
slacks	slăcks	loose-fitting trousers.
taffeta	tăf′ fĕ tȧ	fine, glossy silken fabric.
thread	thrĕad	very thin fine slender cord.
velvet	vĕl′ vĕt	closely woven silk fabric.
voile	voile	dress material of silk or wool.

Refer to a dictionary for definition, pronunciation, and use of:

button,   calico,   chenille,   crash,   pongee.

There are many odd laws in the United States. Very few of them are actually enforced. Some were enacted to meet situations that no longer exist. For instance, there is a law in one of the eastern states that requires a railway company to provide for a man to walk with a lantern in front of a train traveling at night.

In a western state there is a law that forbids the eating of reptiles or scorpions.

Pertaining to Dry Goods

alpaca	ăl păe′ á	cloth made of wool and silk.
bleaching	blēach′ ĭng	process of making white.
buckle	bŭck′ le	instrument for fastening.
buckram	bŭck′ răm	very stiff, coarse canvas.
chintz	chĭntz (chĭnts)	printed cotton cloth.
cretonne	ᴇrē tŏnne′	strong, unglazed cotton cloth.
crochet	ᴇrŏ çhᴇt′	knit with a hooked needle.
doily	doi′ lў	small table napkin.
fabric	făb′ rĭe	woven or knitted material.
flannel	flăn′ nĕl	soft, woven woolen cloth.
foulard	foͅu lärd′	fabric having a satin finish.
girdle	gir′ dle (gûr)	sash or belt for the waist.
gossamer	gŏs′ sá mēr	very thin, gauzelike fabric.
lining	lĭn′ ĭng	covering of the inner surface.
napkin	năp′ kĭn	small cloth used at mealtime.
pattern	păt′ tērn	model for making things.
plaid	plăɪd	checkered woolen cloth.
poplin	pŏp′ lĭn	fabric with a corded surface.
rayon	rāy′ ŏn	material resembling silk.
satin	săt′ ĭn	closely woven, glossy silk.
selvage	sĕl′ vage (vĭj)	edge of a woven fabric.
serge	sērǵe	twilled worsted cloth.
textile	tĕx′ tĭle	fabric made by weaving.
tweed	twēēd	twilled woolen fabric.
yarn	yärn	spun wool or cotton.

Refer to a dictionary for definition, pronunciation, and use of:

collar,   **damask,**   **lisle,**   **sash,**   **twill.**

Silent letters have several uses. They may be used to indicate pronunciation; as, *fade* (fad), *made* (mad), *guilt* (gilt), *road* (rode), mane (man), *ripe* (rip), *sign* (sin), and the like.

It is said that silent letters are the ghosts of departed sounds.

An *arena* is a place for a combat or exertion of any kind. It is derived from a Latin word meaning "sand." This is because the place for combats was covered with sand to absorb the blood of the contestants.

LESSON 50

Architectural and Building Terms

alcove	ăl′ cōv*e*	recess at the side of a room.
arcade	är cād*e*′	arched and roofed gallery.
architect	är′ *ch*ĭ tĕct	person who plans buildings.
attic	ăt′ tĭ*e*	space next to the roof.
auditorium	au dĭ tō′ rĭ ŭm	audience room for the public.
chimney	chĭm′ nĕў	passage for conveying smoke.
concrete	cŏn′ crēt*e*	mixture of sand and cement.
corridor	cŏr′ rĭ dôr	long passageway; hallway.
eaves	ēav*e*ş	projecting edge of a roof.
gable	gā′ bl*e*	triangular end of a building.
grille	grĭll*e*	ornamental lattice work.
jamb	jămb	upright side of a doorway.
keystone	kēỹ′ stōn*e*	middle stone of an arch.
mantel	măn′ t*e*l	beam above a fireplace.
masonry	mā′son rў	work of a builder in stone.
molding	mōld′ ĭng	ornamental border.
newel	new′ ĕl	post supporting stair rail.
portico	pōr′ tĭ cō	colonnade or covered porch.
rafter	råft′ẽr	beam supporting a roof.
rotunda	rŏ tŭn′ då	circular building or wall.
siding	sīd′ ĭng	outside covering of a house.
specification	spĕç ĭ fĭ cā′ tion	written statement of details.
structure	strŭc′ tų̆r*e*	anything that is built.
studding	stŭd′ dĭng	upright beams in a wall.
trestle	trĕs′ *t*l*e*	movable frame or support.

Refer to a dictionary for definition, pronunciation, and use of:

pantry,   pilaster,   rubble,   tiling,   timber.

Words discriminated. Estimate, estimation, appraise. An *estimate* is an approximate calculation in a general way of the worth, extent, or value of property; as, an estimate on the cost of painting a house. *Estimation* is a feeling of respect, esteem, honor, or regard; as, the stenographer stands high in the estimation of the firm. *Appraise* is to set a value on goods, land, or other property.

Architectural and Building Terms

aisle	*aïsle*	passageway in a church.
balcony	băl′ e̊o nў	gallery inside of a building.
basement	bāse′ mĕnt	story partly below ground.
building	buĭld′ ĭng	edifice of any kind.
cement	çĕ mĕnt′	superior kind of mortar.
chamber	chām′ bĕr	room used for sleeping.
dentils	dĕn′ tĭls̗	small blocks in a series.
foundation	foun dā′ tion	base on which a building rests.
girder	gĭr′ dĕr	strong supporting beam.
joists	joists	timbers supporting a floor.
lattice	lăt′ tĭçe	network of wood or metal.
lavatory	lăv′ a̍ tō rў	basin or bowl for washing.
lumber	lŭm′ bĕr	timber sawed ready for market.
mortar	môr′ tăr	mixed lime, sand, and water.
partition	pär tĭ′ tion	interior dividing wall.
plaster	plȧs′ tĕr	mixture for covering walls.
plumbing	plŭm*b*′ ĭng	installing pipes and fixtures.
scantling	seǎnt′ lĭng	timber, usually 2x4 inches.
sheathing	shēa̱ṯẖ′ ĭng	boards used for boxing.
shingles	shĭŋ′ gles̗	thin, short roofing boards.
stucco	stŭe′ e̊ō	exterior coat of cement.
transom	trăn′ so̍m	small window above a door.
veneered	vĕ nēēred′	overlaid with a finer wood.
veranda	vĕ răn′ da̍	open balcony or portico.
vestibule	vĕs′ tĭ būle	passage or entrance way.

Refer to a dictionary for definition, pronunciation, and use of:

coping, cornice, corrugated, mullion, wainscot.

Silent letters are useful to show the meaning of words; as, *whose* and *hose*, *guilt* and *gilt*, *clime* and *climb*, *plume* and *plumb*, *belle* and *bell*, *road* and *rode*, *write* and *right*.

The letters that are never silent are, *f*, *j*, *q*, single *r*, *x*, and the letters representing the sound *sh*.

The word *college* does not have a "d." Compare with *knowledge*.

Hardware Vocabulary

bevel	běv′ ĕl	instrument for marking angles.
bucket	bŭck′ ĕt	pail for carrying water.
butts	bŭtts	small door hinges.
calipers	eăl′ ĭ pērş	measuring compasses.
carborundum	eär bŏ rŭn′ dŭm	hard abrasive compound.
cutlery	eŭt′ lēr y̆	edged or cutting tools.
enameled	ĕn ăm′ ĕled	covered with a lacquer.
faucet	fau′ çĕt (fô)	fixture for drawing liquids.
galvanized	găl′ và nīzed	metals coated with zinc.
gauge *or* **gage**	gãuǵe	instrument used for measuring.
gouge	gouǵe	chisel with a curved edge.
handsaw	hănd′ sąw	saw for use in one hand.
knob	knŏb	round handle of a door.
malleable	măl′ lĕ à ble	pliable; adaptable.
nozzle	nŏz′ zle	short tube attached to a pipe or hose.
pincers	pĭn′ çērş	device used for gripping.
razor	rā′ zŏr	tool for removing the beard.
rivets	rĭv′ ĕts	short-headed pins or bolts.
scissors	scĭş′ şŏrş	two-bladed cutting instrument.
shovel	shŏv′ el	tool used for moving dirt.
sickle	sĭck′ le	tool used for cutting grass.
skillet	skĭl′ lĕt	shallow frying pan.
toaster	tõast′ ēr	device for browning bread.
trowel	trow′ ĕl	tool for spreading mortar.
wrench	wrĕnch	tool used for turning nuts.

Refer to a dictionary for definition, pronunciation, and use of:

bronze,   instruments,   solder,   tweezers,   wedge.

A *primitive* word is a word not derived from any other word in the same language; as, *home, good, man, hot, work.* Two or more primitive words are sometimes combined to form compound words; as, *rainbow, nevertheless.*

There is no such word as "alright."

Quiz, a preliminary or partial examination, is of uncertain origin.

Hardware Vocabulary

aluminum	å lū′ mĭ nŭm	silver-white malleable metal.
auger	au′ gẽr	tool used for boring holes.
cable	eā′ ble	large, strong rope or chain.
canister	eăn′ ĭs tẽr	small box for tea, coffee, etc.
cleaver	elēav′ ẽr	small ax for cutting meat.
compasses	eŏm′ påss ĕş	tool for drawing circles.
funnel	fŭn′ nĕl	vessel the shape of a cone.
gimlet	gĭm′ lĕt	small tool for boring holes.
grindstone	grĭnd′ stōne	stone for grinding tools.
hammer	hăm′ mẽr	tool used for driving nails.
hardware	härd′ wâre	articles made from metals.
hatchet	hă*t*ch′ ĕt	ax-like hammer.
hone	hōne	stone for sharpening tools.
isinglass	ī′ şĭŋ glåss	transparent mica sheets.
lever	lē′ vẽr	bar for lifting weights.
mallet	măl′ lĕt	small wooden hammer.
mattock	măt′ tŏck	tool used for grubbing.
nippers	nĭp′ pẽrş	small pincers for holding.
padlock	păd′lŏck	portable lock with a bow.
percolator	pẽr′ eð lā tõr	coffee pot with a filter.
pliers	plī′ ẽrş	pinchers for bending wire.
screws	serewş (skrōōş)	small threaded bolts.
tongs	tŏngş	implement for holding objects.
washer	wạsh′ ẽr	ring used to relieve friction.
wringer	*w*rĭng′ ẽr	machine to press out water.

Refer to a dictionary for definition, pronunciation, and use of:

emery,   **knives,**   **ladle,**   **level,**   **pumice.**

A *derivative* word is a word formed from some other word by changing it, or by adding a prefix or suffix, or both, so as to modify the meaning of the word; as, *great, greatness; boy, boyish; man, unmanly; reform, reformer.*

Note that the word *balance* has only one *l.* Compare this word with *ballast* and *balloon.*

Meat is a term often applied to food in general. By removing the first letter we have "eat."

"A Day in Court"

accused	ăe eūʂed′	one charged with a crime.
acquittal	ăe quĭt′ tăl	finding of not guilty.
adult	à dŭlt′	person of full legal age.
affirm	ăf fĭrm′	make a solemn declaration.
bequest	bĕ quĕst′	gift of property by will.
civil	çĭv′ ĭl	distinguished from criminal.
collusion	eŏl lū′ sion (zhŭn)	wrongful secret agreement.
conviction	eŏn vĭe′ tion	finding one guilty of a crime.
custody	eŭs′ tŏ dy̆	legal safe-keeping.
equity	ĕq′ uĭ ty̆	natural right or justice.
eviction	ĕ vĭe′ tion	expulsion of an occupant.
exonerate	ĕx̱ ŏn′ ĕr āte	free from a claim or charge.
guilty	guĭlt′ y̆	involving or showing guilt.
indictment	ĭn dīct′ mĕnt	formal written accusation.
innocence	ĭn′ nŏ çĕnçe	freedom from blame or guilt.
justice	jŭs′ tĭçe	quality of being fair.
merger	mĕr′ ġĕr	combination of businesses.
obligation	ŏb lĭ gā′ tion	specific enforceable duty.
ouster	ous′ tĕr	ejection from real property.
perjury	pĕr′ jû ry̆	violation of an oath.
proof	prōof	establishment of a fact.
proximate	prŏx′ ĭ mate (mĭt)	near by; side by side.
retroactive	rĕ trŏ ăe′ tĭve	affecting that which is past.
revoke	rĕ vōke′	annul by taking back.
verdict	vĕr′ dĭet	decision of a jury.

Refer to a dictionary for definition, pronunciation, and use of:

acknowledgment,   bequeath,   code,   intestate,   officer.

Every person is entitled to have his day in court.—

—Legal maxim.

The word *lunatic* is derived from a Latin word, *luna*, meaning the "moon." It literally means "one affected by the moon." It was thought at one time that the unsoundness of the mind was due to the effect of sleeping with the moon shining full on the face, and that the changes in the moon caused changes to take place in the mind of the afflicted person. What is the meaning and cause of being "moonstruck"? Is it possible those primitive people may have been right?

Crimes and Criminals

abscond	ăb seŏnd'	flee to avoid arrest.
accessory	ăe çĕs' sŏ rў	one who assists in a crime.
accomplice	ăe eŏm' plĭçe	associate in a crime.
alibi	ăl' ĭ bī	legal excuse.
arrest	ăr rĕst'	taking a person into custody.
assault	ăs sạult'	unlawful violent attack.
bigamy	bĭg' à mў	having more than one spouse.
bribery	brīb' ēr ў	corruptly influencing another.
burglary	bûr' glà rў	crime of housebreaking.
circumstantial	çĭr eŭm stăn' tial (shăl)	depending upon incidents.
confession	eŏn fĕs' sion	admission of a wrong or crime.
convict	eŏn vĭet'	prove guilty of a crime.
criminal	erĭm' ĭ năl	one who violates the law.
embezzlement	ĕm bĕz' zle mĕnt	diverting money fraudulently.
felony	fĕl' ŏ nў	heinous or capital crime.
forgery	fôr' ġēr ў	making false alterations.
fugitive	fū' ġĭ tĭve	fleeing from duty or pursuit.
gambling	găm' blĭng	playing for stakes or money.
larceny	lär' çĕ nў	unlawfully taking property.
misdemeanor	mĭs dĕ mēan' ŏr	offense less than a felony.
parole	pà rōle'	conditional pardon.
prisoner	prĭṣ' on ēr	one who is deprived of liberty.
robbery	rŏb' bēr ў	feloniously taking property.
vagrant	vā' grănt	having no settled abode.
warrant	wạr' rănt	writ authorizing an arrest.

Refer to a dictionary for definition, pronunciation, and use of:

alias,   **counsel,**   **culprit,**   **reprieve,**   **weapon.**

Crimes are usually classified according to the nature of the punishment as *felonies* and *misdemeanors*. A *felony* is a crime punishable by death or by imprisonment in a penitentiary. A *misdemeanor* is a crime punishable by a fine or by imprisonment in a county jail, or by both a fine and a prison sentence. The statutes declare what acts are felonies and those that are misdemeanors.

63

Mathematical Terms

angle	ăŋ′ gle	figure formed by two lines.
circle	çĭr′ ele	round plane figure.
decimal	dĕç′ ĭ măl	reckoning by tens.
diameter	dī ăm′ ĕ tẽr	width of a circular object.
divide	dĭ vīde′	separate into parts.
equal	ē′ quăl	same size, number, value.
explain	ĕx plāin′	make clear or intelligible.
exponent	ĕx pō′ nĕnt	index of a power, as in a^3.
half	hälf	one of two equal parts.
hundred	hŭn′ drĕd	product of ten times ten.
infinity	ĭn fĭn′ ĭ tў	without extent or bounds.
integer	ĭn′ tĕ ġẽr	whole number, as 1, 2, 3.
length	lĕngth	extent from end to end.
measurement	meas′ ure mĕnt (mĕzh′ ẽr)	result of measuring something.
median	mē′ dĭ ăn	statistical average.
minuend	mĭn′ ũ ĕnd	number to be subtracted from.
multiple	mŭl′ tĭ ple	number exactly divisible.
notation	nŏ tā′ tion	method of writing numbers.
perpendicular	pẽr pĕn dĭe′ ũ lãr	exactly upright or vertical.
problem	prŏb′ lĕm	something to be solved.
quarter	quạr′ tẽr	fourth part of anything.
quotient	quō′ tient (shĕnt)	result obtained by division.
radius	rā′ dĭ ŭs	semidiameter.
segment	sĕg′ mĕnt	part cut off or set off.
tangent	tăn′ ġĕnt	line just touching a curve.

Refer to a dictionary for definition, pronunciation, and use of:

discount,   **norm,**   **square,**   **theory,**   **triangle.**

Words discriminated. Additional, extra, surplus, excess. Additional is applied to something extra; as, an additional sum of money. *Extra* applies to something more than expected or customary. *Surplus* means more than sufficient; as, there is a surplus of revenue. *Excess* refers to that which passes limits; as, an excess of baggage.

Arithmetical Vocabulary

LESSON 57

aliquot
analysis
answer
area
arithmetic
avoirdupois
axis
calculation
cancellation
cipher
column
composite
computation
degree
denomination
denominator
digit
dimension
diminish
diminution
dividend
division
equation
equivalent
evolution

LESSON 58

example
explanation
factoring
figure
forty
fourth
fraction
gallon
graph
horizontal
hundredth
integral
involution
isosceles
linear
magnitude
mensuration
metric
million
minus
multiplicand
multiplication
multiplier
naught
ninetieth

LESSON 59

ninth
number
numeral
numerator
numerical
percentage
perimeter
process
product
progression
proportion
quantity
ratio
reciprocal
reckon
rectangle
reduction
remainder
solution
subtraction
subtrahend
symbol
twelfth
twelve
vertical

Arithmetic is the science of numbers, and the art of computing or reckoning by the use of positive real numbers.

Algebra is the science of calculation by means of letters and other symbols in which the letters express quantities and the signs express operations.

Geometry is that branch of mathematics which treats of forms, magnitudes, measurements, and relations of lines, angles, surfaces, and solids.

Trigonometry is that mathematical science which treats of the relations of the angles and the sides of triangles.

Calculus is a highly systematic method of treating problems by the use of algebraic notations.

65

Words Associated with Losses and Gains

accruals	ăe ᵉrụ′ ălş	something that has increased.
acquisition	ăe quĭ şĭ′ tion	act of accumulating.
advantageous	ăd văn tā′ ǥeoŭs	favorable or profitable.
audit	au′ dĭt	examination of accounts.
bereaved	bĕ rēaᵥed′	deprived of something beloved.
compensation	ᵉŏm pĕn sā′ tion	making up for a loss suffered.
deprivation	dĕp rĭ vā′ tion	state of being deprived; want.
destruction	dĕ strŭe′ tion	widespread damage; devastation.
dispossessed	dĭs pŏş şĕssed′	ejected; put out of possession.
frugality	frụ găl′ ĭ tў	thrift or rigid economy.
gainful	gāin′ fụl	profitable.
insolvency	ĭn sŏl′ vĕn çў	inability to pay just debts.
irredeemable	ĭr rĕ dēēm′ å ble	hopelessly irreclaimable.
losses	lŏss′ ĕş	decreases in proprietorship.
lucre	lū′ ᵉrₑ (kĕr)	profit; riches; money.
money	mȯn′ ₑў	medium of exchange; coinage.
ousted	oust′ ĕd	ejected; removed; evicted.
pecuniary	pĕ eū′ nĭ ar ў (ĕr)	pertaining to money.
privation	prī vā′ tion	want; hardship; dire need.
procure	prŏ eūrₑ′	get; obtain; bring about.
remunerative	rĕ mū′ nẽr ā tĭᵥe	profitable; gainful.
riches	rĭch′ ĕş	abundant means; wealth.
riddance	rĭd′ dănçe	act of clearing away; relief.
swindle	swĭn′ dlₑ	cheat; defraud.
winnings	wĭn′ nĭngş	that which is gained.

Refer to a dictionary for definition, pronunciation, and use of:

crisis,   disaster,   gratuity,   prodigal,   surrender.

Pecuniary is from the Latin, *pecus*, meaning cattle, especially sheep. In early times the Romans did their trading, using as a medium of barter and standard of value both sheep and oxen. Ancient coins were marked with the image of a sheep or ox. They were worth about sixteen cents. That was before the time of the dole and the high cost of living.

Words Relating to Excess, Extravagance, and Expenditure

abundance	à bŭn′ dănçe	more than enough; plentiful.
adequate	ăd′ ē quate (kwĭt)	equal to all needs; enough.
amortize	à môr′ tīze	provide for future payments.
avarice	ăv′ à rĭçe	eager desire for gain.
delinquent	dĕ lĭŋ′ quĕnt	failing to meet an obligation.
disburse	dĭs bûrse′	pay out or expend money.
dissipate	dĭs′ sĭ pāte	squander without any benefit.
dollar	dŏl′ lăr	one hundred cents in money.
exorbitance	ĕx̱ ôr′ bĭ tănçe	excess beyond fair limits.
expenditure	ĕx pĕnd′ ĭ t̰ụre	act of expending; outlay.
expense	ex pĕnse′	operating cost; money spent.
extravagant	ĕx trăv′ à gănt	exceeding reasonable limits.
improvident	ĭm prŏv′ ĭ dĕnt	lacking in foresight or thrift.
lavish	lăv′ ĭsh	waste; spend money foolishly.
misspend	mĭs spĕnd′	spend for a wrong purpose.
niggardly	nĭg′ gärd lў	miserly; stingy.
overcharge	ō vēr chärġe′	ask too high a price.
participate	pär tĭç′ ĭ pāte	take part or share with others.
penurious	pĕ nū′ rĭ oŭs	very sparing; parsimonious.
pittance	pĭt′ tănçe	small allowance of money.
spendthrift	spĕnd′ thrĭft	prodigal spender of money.
squander	squa̱n′ dēr	spend lavishly or wastefully.
stinginess	stĭn′ ġĭ nĕss	niggardliness.
stint	stĭnt	provide scantily; limit.
wasteful	wāste′ fụl	causing waste; destructive.

Refer to a dictionary for definition, pronunciation, and use of:

expend,   indigence,   luxury,   stipend,   profuse.

Spelling: Should the word "double" be used in oral spelling? It is a disputed question among the authorities whether the oral speller should repeat double letters or use the word "double"; as *b, l, o, o, m, bloom*; or *b, l, double-o, m, bloom*. Both methods are in use by teachers, individual preferences being the determining factor, with the probability that the first way is becoming the more popular.

Words Pertaining to Time and Seasons

anniversary	ăn nĭ vēr′ sả rў	annual return of the day of a past event.
annual	ăn′ nủ ăl	occurring every year.
autumn	au′ tŭm*n*	commonly called *fall* in America.
century	çĕn′ tụ rў	period of one hundred years.
daily	dā*i*′ lў	happening every day.
decade	dĕe′ āde	ten consecutive years.
epoch	ĕp′ ŏe*h*	interval of time; era, or age.
eternity	ē tēr′ nĭ tў	endless duration of time.
February	Fĕb′ rụ ar ў (ĕr)	second month in the year.
forenoon	fōre nōōn′	early part of the day.
Friday	Frī′ da ў	sixth day of the week.
future	fū′ tụre	time yet to come.
immediately	ĭm mē′ dĭ ate lў (ĭt)	at once or without delay.
instant	ĭn′ stănt	any particular time; a moment.
intermission	ĭn tēr mĭs′ sion	intervening period of time.
modern	mŏd′ ērn	recent; present.
month	mȯnth	twelfth part of a year.
perpetual	pēr pĕt′ụ ăl	continuing without stopping.
postpone	pōst pōne′	put off; defer; delay.
seasons	sēa′ şonş	divisions of a year.
senior	sēn′ ior (yēr)	one older than another.
tardiness	tär′ dĭ nĕss	lateness.
Wednesday	Wednes′ da ў (Wĕnz′)	fourth day of the week.
weekly	wēēk′ lў	occurring once each week.
yesterday	yĕs′ tēr da ў	day before today.

Refer to a dictionary for definition, pronunciation, and use of:

always,   frequently,   interval,   noontide,   prior.

Eternity has to do with infinite duration. There are three eternities. First, there is the eternity of the past. Second, there is an eternity of the future. Third, there is an eternity of space.

By the addition of the letter *t* to the word *here* we get the opposite meaning of the word; as, *there*.

Labor and Capital

agency	ā′ ġĕn çў	business of acting for another.
artisan	är′ tĭ şăn	one skilled in mechanical arts.
consumer	eŏn sūm′ ẽr	one who buys and uses goods.
co-operate	eŏ-ŏp′ ẽr āte	act or join with others.
craftsman	eräfts′ măn	skilled mechanic or artisan.
drudgery	drŭdġ′ ẽr ў	wearisome work or labor.
economize	ĕ eŏn′ ŏ mīze	utilize to advantage; save.
employer	ĕm ploy′ ẽr	one who hires another.
extortion	ĕx tôr′ tion	obtaining money by force.
federation	fĕd ẽr ā′ tion	union of different bodies.
investor	ĭn vĕs′ tõr	one who invests money for gain.
journeyman	joûr′ neў măn	one who has learned a trade.
laborious	là bō′ rĭ oŭs	with much toil; arduous.
magnate	măg′ nāte	person of great wealth.
mechanic	mĕ ehăn′ ĭe	skilled worker; an artificer.
mediate	mē′ dĭ āte	effect a reconciliation.
monopolize	mŏ nŏp′ ŏ līze	acquire an exclusive control.
organize	ôr′ găn īze	unite and work together.
ownership	ōwn′ ẽr shĭp	legal title or proprietorship.
poverty	pŏv′ ẽr tў	want; destitution.
producer	prŏ dūç′ ẽr	one who makes goods or renders services.
prosperity	prŏs pĕr′ ĭ tў	material well-being.
restraint	rĕ strāint′	hindrance or restriction.
toiler	toil′ ẽr	hard worker or laborer.
tyranny	tўr′ àn nў	despotic exercise of power.

Refer to a dictionary for definition, pronunciation, and use of:

blacklist,   masses,   rivalry,   society,   thrift.

Comma.—The comma is a mark of punctuation (,) extensively used in all sorts of composition to indicate only a slight pause, or to indicate a slight break in the continuity of ideas or construction. Some writers use commas profusely and in such a case the punctuation is said to be *close.* When commas are not considered absolutely necessary and are omitted, the punctuation is said to be *open.*

Trades, Occupations, and Professions

LESSON 64	LESSON 65	LESSON 66
artist	expressman	peddler
assayer	farmer	pharmacist
auctioneer	fireman	photographer
banker	florist	physician
barber	furrier	plasterer
brakeman	gardener	plumber
caterer	glazier	porter
chemist	interpreter	printer
cobbler	janitor	reformer
compositor	jeweler	salesman
confectioner	lather	seaman
contractor	laundress	servant
decorator	lawyer	solicitor
demonstrator	lecturer	stationer
dentist	librarian	stenographer
designer	machinist	stereotyper
doctor	manicurist	superintendent
draftsman	mason	surgeon
dressmaker	merchant	tailor
druggist	messenger	telegrapher
editor	minister	tinner
educator	oculist	typist
electrician	optician	upholsterer
engraver	osteopath	veterinarian
evangelist	painter	waitress

Consult a dictionary for definition, pronunciation, and use of:

artisan,   laity,   occupation,   professional,   tradesman.

Each shall follow with cheerfulness the profession which he best understands.

—Horace.

Seest thou a man diligent in his business? He shall stand before kings and not mean men.

—Solomon.

There be no greater blessing in this world than a steady job, with increasing efficiency and, hence, increasing wages as time goes on.

—Paul H. Hanus.

LESSON 67

Pertaining to Music

accompani-	ăe ĕȯm′ på nĭ mĕnt	music supporting a singer.
ment		
anthem	ăn′ thĕm	song of praise or gladness.
cantata	eăn tä′ tȧ	poem or drama set to music.
choir	choir (kwīr)	organized body of singers.
concert	eŏn′ çĕrt	public musical performance.
cornet	eȏr′ nĕt	horn-shaped wind instrument.
duet	dŭ ĕt′	selection for two performers.
encore	en′ eōre (äN′)	call or demand for repetition.
guitar	guĭ tär′	six-stringed instrument.
harmony	här′ mȯ nў	agreeable blending of tones.
lullaby	lŭll′ ȧ bȳ	soothing cradle song.
melody	mĕl′ ȯ dў	tunefulness; harmony.
musician	mŭ si′ ciăn (zĭsh)	skilled player or singer.
opera	ŏp′ ĕr ȧ	drama set to music.
oratorio	ŏr ȧ tō′ rĭ ō	sacred musical composition.
orchestra	ȏr′ eĕs trȧ	group of musical performers.
overture	ō′ vĕr t̰ụre	orchestral composition.
pianist	pĭ ăn′ ĭst	skilled piano player.
recital	rĕ çīt′ ăl	program of music.
rehearsal	rĕ hĕars′ ăl	practice for a performance.
serenade	sĕr ĕ nāde′	music in the open air at night.
soprano	sȯ prä′ nō	highest quality of a voice.
symphony	sўm′ phȯ nў	harmonious blending of sounds.
tenor	tĕn′ ȏr	highest adult male voice.
violin	vī ȯ lĭn′	four-stringed instrument.

Refer to a dictionary for definition, pronunciation, and use of:

baton,   carol,   melodious,   saxophone,   vocal.

Learning to spell:—Without doubt, it is not easy—that is, it is not very easy—to learn to spell English. But why should it be easy? It is not easy to learn to do anything rightly and readily that is much worth doing, or to get thoroughly any knowledge that is much worth the knowing. To learn to spell requires attention, observation, application, memory.

—RICHARD GRANT WHITE.

Industrial Arts

abrasive	ăb rā′ sĭv*e*	that which grinds or polishes.
apparatus	ăp pȧ rā′ tŭs	set of tools or instruments.
boring	bōr′ ĭng	act of penetrating.
carpentry	eär′ pĕn trў	art of joining lumber together.
chamfer	chăm′ fer	cut a furrow in; to groove.
countersink	eoun′ tēr sĭnk	chamfer a hole.
crucible	erụ′ çĭ bl*e*	vessel or melting pot.
decorative	dĕe′ ŏ rā tĭv*e*	ornamental.
filing	fīl′ ĭng	sharpening with a file.
forging	fôrġ′ ĭng	heating and shaping metals.
gluing	glụ′ ĭng	joining together with glue.
joinery	join′ ēr ў	things made by a joiner.
lathe	lā*th*e	machine for shaping articles.
machine	mȧ çhĭn*e*′	appliance for performing work.
manual	măn′ ụ ăl	made or done with the hands.
miter	mī′ tēr	slanting or beveled joint.
protractor	prŏ trăe′ tŏr	angle-measuring instrument.
ratchet	ră*t*ch′ ĕt	wheel having angular teeth.
rattan	răt tăn′	long, slender, flexible reed.
shellac	shĕl lăe′	resin used in making varnish.
sloyd	sloyd	system of manual training.
taboret	tăb ŏ rĕt′	seat without arms or back.
tenon	tĕn′ ȯn	that which fits into a mortise.
thumbscrew	thŭm*b*′ serew	made to turn with the thumb.
varnish	vär′ nĭsh	liquid forming a glossy coat.

Refer to a dictionary for definition, pronunciation, and use of:

design,   mortise,   project,   reamer,   welding.

Manual pertains to that which is done by the hand. At one time "making by hand" and manufacture were equivalent terms. They now have a contradictory meaning. A handmade shoe is made by hand, but a manufactured shoe is produced largely by machinery; it is a "machine-made" shoe.

Many educated persons overlook the fact that the last syllable of manual is *al* and not *el*. The proper noun, *Manuel*, ends in *el*.

Pertaining to War

allies	ăl līes′	those leagued with others.
ammunition	ăm mŭ nĭ′ tion	supplies for firearms.
armistice	är′ mĭ stĭçe	temporary cessation of war.
artillery	är tĭl′ lẽr y̆	mounted movable guns; cannon.
battle	băt′ tle	fight between armed forces.
belligerent	bĕl lĭg′ ẽr ĕnt	having to do with war; warlike.
censor	çĕn′ sŏr	one who forbids publication.
cruiser	eruis′ ẽr	war vessel not heavily armed.
deserter	dĕ sẽrt′ ẽr	one who abandons a duty.
furlough	fûr′ lō*ugh*	leave of absence from duty.
hostilities	hŏs tĭl′ ĭ tĭes	acts of warfare; enmities.
insurrection	ĭn sŭr rĕe′ tion	open revolt against authority.
militia	mĭ lĭ′ tiȧ (lĭsh)	citizens enrolled and drilled.
patriot	pā′ trĭ ȯt	lover of one's native country.
rebellion	rĕ bĕl′ lion (yŭn)	open, organized resistance.
recruit	rĕ erų t′	furnish with additional men.
regiment	rĕg′ ĭ mĕnt	organized body of soldiers.
revolution	rĕv ȯ lū′ tion	overthrow of the government.
sentinel	sĕn′ tĭ nĕl	one who watches or guards.
siege	sĭēge	attempt to gain possession.
soldier	sōl′ diẽr (jẽr)	person in military service.
stratagem	străt′ ȧ ġĕm	trick to deceive the enemy.
torpedo	tôr pē′ dō	shell filled with explosives.
veteran	vĕt′ ẽr ăn	one grown old in experience.
volunteer	vŏl ŭn tēēr′	one who enlists voluntarily.

Refer to a dictionary for definition, pronunciation, and use of:

besiege,   capitulate,   morale,   traitor,   truce.

Sentinel, meaning "to watch" or "stand on guard," is probably derived from the French reference to a path or "beat."

Shrapnel is a shell with thin walls containing small round projectiles, with a time fuse for exploding at a given point. It is named in honor of Henry Shrapnel, a British general, who is said to be the inventor.

Espionage refers to a systematic study of the words and conduct of others, especially in a war.

Words Associated with Religion

agnostic	ăg nŏs′ tĭe	one who professes ignorance of nature of God.
atheist	ā′ thĕ ĭst	one who denies the existence of God.
benediction	bĕn ĕ dĭe′ tion	solemn blessing.
catechism	eăt′ ĕ ehĭşm	questions and answers.
cathedral	eà thē′ drăl	principal church of a district.
christen	ehrĭs′ ten	name, as in baptism.
commandment	eŏm mànd′ mĕnt	any one of the Decalogue.
desecration	dĕs ĕ erā′ tion	disrespectful disregard.
disciple	dĭs çī′ ple	learner; follower; adherent.
gentile	ġĕn′ tīle	person who is not Jewish.
hypocrite	hўp′ ŏ erĭte	one who practices deception.
infidel	ĭn′ fĭ dĕl	one without religious faith.
iniquity	ĭn ĭq′ uĭ tў	wickedness; unrighteousness.
irreverence	ĭr rĕv′ ĕr ĕnçe	disregard of things sacred.
parochial	pà rō′ ehĭ ăl	pertaining to a parish.
pastor	pàs′ tŏr	minister in charge of a church.
penitence	pĕn′ ĭ tĕnçe	sorrow for sin; repentance.
profane	prŏ fāne′	wicked; irreverent; impious.
protestant	prŏt′ ĕs tănt	declaring an opposing opinion.
religious	rĕ li′ gious (lĭ′ jŭs)	faithful or conscientious.
repentance	rĕ pĕnt′ ănçe	regret or sorrow for sin.
scoffer	seôff′ ĕr	one who shows contempt.
Scriptures	Serip′ tu̯reş	any sacred writings; the Bible.
sermon	sēr′ mòn	religious discourse.
spiritual	spĭr′ ĭ tu̯ăl	having to do with the soul.

Refer to a dictionary for definition, pronunciation, and use of:

dogma,   piety,   salvation,   skeptic,   testament.

Bible. The word simply means "books"—from the Greek *biblos*, signifying the inner bark of the papyrus. Thus it meant originally any book made of papryus paper. Now the name is confined exclusively to the "Book of Books."

Congregation is an assembly of persons. The original meaning was "a flock or herd." In a symbolic sense, it means "to gather into a flock or a united body." Like birds of a feather we flock together.

74

Words Associated with Religion

baptism	băp′ tĭẓm	ceremony of baptizing.
blasphemy	blăs′ phĕ mў	profanity; irreverent language.
catholic	eăth′ ŏ lĭe	having broad sympathies.
Christian	€hrĭs′ tian (chăn)	professed follower of Christ.
clergyman	eler′ ġў măn	ordained minister or priest.
communicant	eŏm mū′ nĭ eănt	member of a church.
congregation	eŏn grĕ gā′ tion	public assembly of persons.
dedicate	dĕd′ ĭ eāte	set apart for serious purposes.
devotion	dĕ vō′ tion	act of worship; prayer.
divine	dĭ vīne′	pertaining to the Deity.
doctrine	dŏe′ trĭne	tenets of a religious body.
heathen	hēa′ thĕn	irreligious person; pagan.
idolater	ī dŏl′ ȧ tēr	one who worships images.
invocation	ĭn vŏ eā′ tion	prayer or solemn entreaty.
orthodox	ôr′ thŏ dŏx	holding the accepted faith.
pulpit	pụl′ pĭt	elevated stand in a church.
regeneration	rĕ ġĕn ēr ā′ tion	entering into a spiritual life.
religion	rĕ lĭ′ gion (lĭj ŭn)	system of faith or worship.
Sabbath	Săb′ bȧth	appointed day of worship.
sacrilege	săe′ rĭ lĕġe	desecration of things sacred.
solemn	sŏl′ ĕmn	serious; awe-inspiring.
superstitious	sū pēr stĭ′ tious (stĭsh)	fearful of the unknown.
synagogue	sўn′ ȧ gŏgue	place of Jewish worship.
theology	thĕ ŏl′ ŏ ġў	science which treats of God.
worship	wor′ shĭp (wûr)	homage or devotion to God.

Refer to a dictionary for definition, pronunciation, or use of:

bigot,   deity,   diocese,   heresy,   revelation.

Heathen usually refers to a person whose religion is neither Christian, Jewish, nor Mohammedan (though in early use Mohammedans were sometimes called heathens). The word originally referred to a person who lived in the country or on the heath. Christian doctrines could not reach these remote people until long after the doctrines had been accepted in towns and villages.

Health and Sickness

allopathy	ăl lŏp′ á thў	"the old school of medicine."
anemic	á nē′ mĭe	bloodless; lifeless; pale.
anesthetic	ăn ĕs thĕt′ ĭe	drug causing insensibility.
autopsy	au′ tŏp sў	post-mortem examination.
bacteria	băe tē′ rĭ á	small vegetable organisms.
cartilage	eär′ tĭ lage (lĭj)	elastic animal tissue; gristle.
corpuscle	eôr′ pŭs çle	minute cell in the blood.
deleterious	dĕl ĕ tē′ rĭ oŭs	very harmful to life or health.
disinfectant	dĭs ĭn fĕet′ ănt	germ-destroying preparation.
hiccup	hĭe′ eŭp	short, spasmodic cough.
immune	ĭm mūne′	freedom from disease.
inoculate	ĭn ŏe′ û lāte	communicate a disease germ.
insomnia	ĭn sŏm′ nĭ á	inability to sleep.
liniment	lĭn′ ĭ mĕnt	medicine for external use.
malignant	má lĭg′ nănt	tending to cause death.
narcotic	när eŏt′ ĭe	drug that allays pain; opium.
nourishment	noûr′ ĭsh mĕnt	that which gives strength.
operation	ŏp ĕr ā′ tion	surgical treatment.
parasite	păr′ á sīte	organism that lives on others.
pestilence	pĕs′ tĭ lĕnçe	contagious epidemic; plague.
prescription	prĕ serĭp′ tion	written formula or directions.
surgery	sûr′ ġẽr ў	treatment by an operation.
symptom	sўmp′ tóm	change indicating disease.
tonic	tŏn′ ĭe	medicine that gives vigor.
vitamin	vī′ tá mĭn	substance essential to health.

Refer to a dictionary for definition, pronunciation, and use of:

diagnose, hereditary, hypodermic, indigestible, ptomaine.

Chiropractic is a system of treating bodily ailments without the use of drugs by manipulation of the spine by hand or adjusting the joints of the spine. A *chiropractor* is one who practices drugless healing by manipulations of the spine.

Disease literally means "discomfort" or "lack of ease," or "want of ease." It is derived from the Latin *dis*, signifying "apart", and the French *aise*, referring to ease or comfort.

Health and Sickness

abscess	ăb′ scĕss	inflammatory tumor; a boil.
antitoxin	ăn tĭ tŏx′ ĭn	immunizing substance.
cauterize	ҫau′ tẽr īz*e*	burn or sear with a hot iron.
contagious	ҫȯn tā′ gious (jŭs)	communicable by contact.
convalescence	ҫȯn và lĕs′ ҫĕnҫ*e*	gradual recovery of health.
delirium	dĕ lĭr′ ĭ ŭm	wandering of the mind.
epidemic	ĕp ĭ dĕm′ ĭ*e*	afflicting a great number.
fumigate	fū′ mĭ gāt*e*	disinfect by smoke or gas.
hemorrhage	hĕm′ ŏr r*h*age (rĭj)	any discharge of blood.
hygiene	hȳ′ ģiēn*e*	science of healthy living.
incurable	ĭn ҫur′ à bl*e*	not admitting of a remedy.
infection	ĭn fĕҫ′ tion	disease spread by germs.
infirmary	ĭn fĭr′ mà rў	place for care of the sick.
malady	măl′ à dў	lingering disorder or disease.
malaria	mà lâr′ ĭ à	"fever and ague."
massage	màs sage′ (säzh′)	rub, roll, or knead the body.
medicine	mĕd′ ĭ ҫĭn*e*	drug for treating a disease.
nausea	nau′ se a (nô′ shĕ à)	sickness of the stomach.
nostrum	nŏs′ trŭm	quack or patent medicine.
plague	plāg*ue*	deadly spreading disease.
poison	poi′ ṣon	substance that destroys life or health.
respiration	rĕs pĭ rā′ tion	act or process of breathing.
sanitary	săn′ ĭ tăr ў	free from agencies injurious to health.
sterilize	stĕr′ ĭ līz*e*	destroy germs or bacteria.
vaccinate	văҫ′ ҫĭ nāt*e*	inoculate with a vaccine.

Refer to a dictionary for definition, pronunciation, and use of:

antiseptic,   assimilate,   bandage,   clinic,   inflammation.

Asclepius was a Greek god who had two daughters. One of them was called *Hygeia*, the personification of health. From this word we get *hygiene*, the science of the preservation of health, and the system of sanitation. This god's other daughter was called *Panacea* and from this word we get a remedy for all diseases, or a universal medicine or remedy.

Medical Terms

abdomen	ăb dō′ měn	lower part of the body.
abnormal	ăb nôr′ măl	out of the usual course.
adenoids	ăd′ ĕ noidş	spongy tissue; fleshy growth.
amputate	ăm′ pŭ tāt*e*	remove a limb or a portion.
anatomy	ȧ năt′ ŏ mў̆	science of bodily structure.
atrophy	ăt′ rŏ phў̆	drying up or wasting away.
cancer	ĕăn′ çẽr	malignant spreading growth.
canker	ĕăŋ′ kẽr	ulcers in or about the mouth.
cuticle	ĕū′ tĭ ɕl*e*	outer layer of the skin.
dissect	dĭs sĕct′	divide into separate parts.
emaciate	ĕ mā′ ci āt*e* (shĭ)	make lean or thin.
epilepsy	ĕp′ ĭ lĕp sў̆	chronic nervous disorder.
feverish	fē′ vẽr ĭsh	affected with fever; restless.
hysteria	hў̆s tē′ rĭ ȧ	nervous condition.
lassitude	lăs′ sĭ tūd*e*	want of energy; weariness.
microbe	mī′ ɕrōb*e*	minute living organism.
phlegm	phlĕ*g*m	discharge from the throat.
physiology	phў̆ş ĭ ŏl′ ŏ ġў̆	science of living bodies.
pulmonary	pŭl′ mŏ nar ў̆ (nĕr)	pertaining to the lungs.
pulse	pŭls*e*	beating caused by the arteries.
quarantine	quạr′ ăn tïn*e*	restraint upon movement.
serum	sē′ rŭm	watery animal fluid.
tetanus	tĕt′ ȧ nŭs	muscular spasms; lockjaw.
vertebra	vẽr′ tĕ brȧ	small bone of the spine.
virus	vī′ rŭs	morbid poisonous matter.

Refer to a dictionary for definition, pronunciation, and use of:

ague   **health,**   **lethargy,**   **membrane,**   **tumor.**

Homeopathy is the art of curing disease by giving remedies which in a healthy person would produce the symptoms of the disease or complaint of the person, on the principle that "like cures like." The remedies are usually administered in minute doses. The theory of vaccination is a sort of homeopathy by producing in a healthy person a mild form of the disease guarded against. The system of homeopathy was founded by Dr. Samuel Hahnemann.

Common to Drugs

ammonia	ăm mō′ nĭ à	pungent, strong-smelling gas.
anodyne	ăn′ ŏ dȳn*e*	drug that allays pain.
antidote	ăn′ tĭ dōt*e*	remedy to counteract poison.
aromatic	ăr ŏ măt′ ĭ*e*	having a sweet odor; fragrant.
atomizer	ăt′ ȯm īz ẽr	instrument used for spraying.
caffeine	eăf′ fē ĭn*e*	stimulant found in coffee.
calomel	eăl′ ŏ mĕl	preparation of mercury.
capsule	eăp′ sūl*e*	gelatin case for a drug.
codeine	eō′ dĕ ĭn*e*	derivative of morphine.
creosote	erē′ ŏ sōt*e*	antiseptic of smoky odor.
elixir	ĕ lĭx′ ĭr	invigorating substance.
essence	ĕs′ sĕnç*e*	concentrated extract; perfume.
ingredient	ĭn grē′ dĭ ĕnt	component part of a mixture.
listerine	lĭs tẽr ĭn*e*′	patent, antiseptic preparation.
lotion	lō′ tion	liquid healing wash.
lozenge	lŏz′ ĕnǵ*e*	sweet medicated tablet.
naphtha	năph′ thà	inflammable volatile liquid.
nicotine	nĭe′ ŏ tïn*e*	active principle of tobacco.
panacea	păn à çē′ à	remedy for all diseases.
pharmacy	phär′ mà çў	professional drugstore.
quinine	quī′ nīn*e*	bitter drug used as a tonic.
remedy	rĕm′ ĕ dў	medicine that cures diseases.
salve	săl*v*e	soothing, healing ointment.
sassafras	săs′ sà frăs	pungent aromatic bark.
sulphur	sŭl′ phur (fẽr)	yellow mineral; brimstone.

Refer to a dictionary for definition, pronunciation, and use of:

borax,   cathartic,   pomade,   tincture,   vaccine.

Allopathy is that system of treating diseases by endeavoring to combat the complaint by creating a condition of the body contrary to that caused by the disease treated.

Osteopathy is based on the theory that diseases are due chiefly to defects of the skeleton affecting the adjacent nerves and blood vessels. Treatment is directed toward manipulation of the affected area.

Diseases, Drugs, and the Human Body

LESSON 76	LESSON 77	LESSON 78
aconite	gargle	ointment
apoplexy	germicide	opium
appendicitis	glycerin	paralysis
arnica	goiter	phenol
arsenic	hormone	pneumonia
artery	indigestion	poultice
balsam	intestinal	relapse
belladonna	iodine	retina
bilious	iodoform	rheumatism
bronchitis	jaundice	saliva
camphor	knuckle	sciatica
catarrh	laceration	scrofula
chloroform	laudanum	sedative
chronic	laxative	skeleton
cocaine	licorice	spleen
diaphragm	ligament	stimulant
digestion	liver	strychnine
diphtheria	magnesia	thyroid
dyspepsia	measles	tissue
eczema	meningitis	tonsillitis
emetic	menthol	tuberculosis
epidermis	morphine	turpentine
erysipelas	mucous	typhoid
forearm	nasal	ulcer
freckles	neuralgia	vaseline

Calomel is obtained by a mixture of mercury and corrosive sublimate. It is so called because it is white although it is made from dark ingredients. *Mercury* is the only known liquid metal.

Alcohol is a colorless, inflammable liquid obtained by fermentation and distillation. This word comes to us through the Arabic *al-kohl*, a fine powder used to paint the eyebrows and beautify the face. The word is so old in Asia that it may be suspected of reaching back to the Garden of Eden.

Cordial is from the Latin, *cordis*, meaning "the heart." Now it may be a drink that revives and cheers; it may be a medicine that revives; it may mean hearty with friends. The complimentary close of a letter, "Cordially yours," is, therefore, "from the heart."

Pertaining to Chemistry

acetylene	à çĕt′ ў̆ lēn*e*	brilliant, colorless gas.
acid	ăç′ ĭd	sharp or sour to the taste.
alcohol	ăl′ e*ð* hôl	volatile, distilled liquid.
alkaline	ăl′ kà lĭn*e*	neutralizing substance.
alloy	ăl loy′	mixture of base metals.
atom	ăt′ ȯm	anything exceedingly small.
carbon	eär′ bŏn	nonmetallic element.
chemistry	*e*hĕm′ ĭs trў̆	science of the elements.
crystallize	erў̆s′ tăl līz*e*	become fixed in form.
distillation	dĭs tĭl lā′ tion	purification by evaporation.
experiment	ĕx pĕr′ ĭ mĕnt	find out by test or trial.
gaseous	găs′ ĕ o*ŭ*s	having the nature of gas.
hydrogen	hў̄′ dr*ð* ġĕn	lightest known substance.
mercury	mẽr′ e*ŭ* rў̆	liquid metal; quicksilver.
neon	nē′ ŏn	inert gaseous element.
nitrogen	nī′ tr*ð* ġĕn	element forming $\frac{4}{5}$ of the air.
oxygen	ŏx′ ў̆ ġĕn	colorless, inodorous gas.
peroxide	pĕr ŏx′ īd*e*	oxide containing oxygen.
petroleum	pĕ trō′ lĕ ŭm	source of gasoline.
qualitative	quạl′ ĭ tā tĭv*e*	pertaining to the quality.
quantitative	quạn′ tĭ tā tĭv*e*	concerned with the quantity.
radium	rā′ dĭ ŭm	rare metallic element.
sodium	sō′ dĭ ŭm	soft, waxy, silver-white metal.
substance	sŭb′ stănç*e*	that from which a thing is made.
volatile	vŏl′ à tĭl*e*	power to evaporate quickly.

Refer to a dictionary for definition, pronunciation, and use of:

compound,   liquefy,   organic,   reaction,   soluble.

Chemistry was originally confined to the art of extracting juices from plants for medical purposes. The chemists of the Middle Ages were known as *alchemists*. The great objective of these medieval chemists was the transmuting of the baser metals into gold and silver, and the discovery of a universal cure for all diseases with the hope of prolonging life indefinitely. Out of this practice many important discoveries were made, from which evolved the modern science of chemistry.

Pertaining to Physics

acceleration	ăe çĕl ĕr ā′ tion	act of increasing speed.
barometer	bȧ rŏm′ ĕ tẽr	air-pressure measurement.
cohesion	eŏ hē′ sion (zhŭn)	attraction that unites bodies.
density	dĕn′ sĭ tў	quality of being dense.
electron	ē lĕe′ trŏn	minute electrified particle.
expansion	ĕx păn′ sion	increase in size or scope.
friction	frĭe′ tion	rubbing together of two bodies.
fulcrum	fŭl′ erŭm	point of support for a lever.
gravitation	grăv ĭ tā′ tion	force drawing bodies together.
humidity	hŭ mĭd′ ĭ tў	condition of the atmosphere.
hydraulic	hȳ drau′ lĭe	conveying or operated by water.
inertia	ĭn ẽr′ ti a (shȧ)	tendency to remain at rest.
kilowatt	kĭl′ ŏ wạtt	unit of electrical power.
magnetism	măg′ nĕt ĭşm	power of attraction.
matter	măt′ tẽr	that which occupies space.
molecule	mŏl′ ĕ eūle	any minute particle.
optics	ŏp′ tĭes	science that treats of vision.
physics	phў̆s′ ĭes	laws and properties of matter.
radiation	rā dĭ ā′ tion	diffusion of rays into space.
refraction	rĕ frăe′ tion	change in direction of a ray.
temperature	tĕm′ pẽr ȧ t̪u̪re	measurement of heat or cold.
thermometer	thẽr mŏm′ ĕ tẽr	heat measuring instrument.
translucent	trăns lū′ çĕnt	imperfectly transparent.
vacuum	văe ′ ŭ ŭm	perfectly empty space.
velocity	vĕ lŏç′ ĭ tў	speed at which a thing moves.

Refer to a dictionary for definition, pronunciation, and use of:

acoustics,   gravity,   pendulum,   siphon,   watt.

Relativity (in physics) is a theory formulated by Einstein that all motion is relative, denying the existence of gravitation. The theory is so abstruse that it is said only few persons can understand it thoroughly.

Physics is the science of matter and natural objects. It is derived from *physic*, "a knowledge of man's nature." In time *physic* came to mean "the science and practice of medicine," and later "a drug or medicine." Shapespeare said: "I will have none of it."

Electrical Terms

alternating	ạl′ tẽr nāt ĭng	take or follow in turn.
ammeter	ăm′ mē tẽr	current-measuring instrument.
ampere	ăm′ pēre	unit of electrical current.
anode	ăn′ ōde	positive pole of a battery.
armature	är′ mȧ ṯụre	part of an electric motor.
automatic	au tŏ măt′ ĭe	power of acting in itself.
cathode	eăth′ ōde	negative electric pole.
circuit	çĭr′ euĭt	path of an electric current.
coherer	eŏ hēr′ ẽr	signal detecting device.
condenser	eŏn dĕns′ ẽr	electric concentrating device.
conduit	eŏn′ duĭt	inclosed tube for wires.
copper	eŏp′ pẽr	red tenacious metal.
ductility	dŭe tĭl′ ĭ tỹ	flexibility; pliableness.
dynamo	dȳ′ nȧ mō	electric-current generator.
elasticity	ē lăs tĭç′ ĭ tỹ	power to regain shape.
electricity	ē lĕe trĭç′ ĭ tỹ	undefined molecular force.
fuse	fūṣe	melt by means of heat.
galvanic	găl văn′ ĭe	producing electrical current.
incandescent	ĭn eăn dĕs′ çĕnt	glowing with white heat.
insulator	ĭn′ sŭ lā tŏr	nonconducting substance.
magneto	măg nē′ tō	current-generating mechanism.
rheostat	rhē′ ŏ stăt	current-regulating device.
tenacious	tĕ nā′ cious (shŭs)	sticking together very tightly.
tungsten	tŭng′ stĕn	metal used to make filaments.
volt	vōlt	unit of electrical force.

Refer to a dictionary for definition, pronunciation, and use of:

ether,   generator,   induction,   ohm,   vibrator.

Ether is a colorless and pleasant-smelling compound. Its chief use is as an anesthetic, having qualities making it preferable to chloroform. The literal meaning of the word is "the upper air." In the science of physics ether is supposed to be a medium that fills all space, even those portions occupied by fluids and solids. The ancient philosophers held that ether was the air breathed by the gods.

Motor Vehicles

accessories	ăe çĕs' sŏ rĭeş	additional subordinate parts.
automobile	au tŏ mŏ bïle'	self-propelling vehicle.
carburetor	cär' bŭ rĕt ōr	gas and air mixing apparatus.
chassis	çhăs' sĭs	main frame of an automobile.
chauffeur	çhauf feur' (shŏ fûr')	automobile operator for pay.
clutch	elŭtch	device for gripping two parts.
coupe	eoụpẹ'	inclosed car with one seat.
detour	dĕ toụr'	roundabout road; deviation.
fender	fĕnd' ẽr	guard for the wheel.
garage	gà rage' (räzh')	place for housing automobiles.
gasket	găs' kĕt	packing for a joint or piston.
gasoline	găs' ŏ lïne	liquid obtained from petroleum.
ignition	ĭg nĭ' tion	process of exploding gasoline.
muffler	mŭf' flẽr	noise deadening device.
pneumatic	pneŭ mắt' ĭe	having to do with air.
puncture	pŭŋẹ' tụre	small hole in the tire.
reverse	rĕ vẽrsẹ'	backward motion; opposite.
roadster	rōad' stẽr	automobile with an open body.
runabout	rŭn' à bout	one-seated light roadster.
skidding	skĭd' dĭng	sliding sidewise.
speedometer	spēēd ŏm' ĕ tẽr	instrument indicating speed.
taxicab	tăx' ĭ eăb	motor vehicle for hire.
tonneau	tôn neau' (nō')	rounded rear section of car.
tractor	trăe' tŏr	automobile used for hauling.
vulcanize	vŭl' eăn īze	treat rubber by chemical means.

Refer to a dictionary for definition, pronunciation, and use of:

accelerator,   gadget,   piston,   transmission,   valve.

Words discriminated. Implement, instrument, tool, utensil. We speak of the machinery used by a farmer as *implements.* A dentist uses *instruments;* a carpenter, *tools;* and a housewife, *utensils* (for cooking). A tool is understood to be smaller than an implement or instrument. A mixing bowl is an illustration of a utensil.

Aviation

aeronaut	ā′ ēr ô naut	aerial operator or rider.
aileron	āi′ lēr ŏn	small balancing plane.
aircraft	âir′ erȧft	flying machines of all kinds.
airdrome	âir′ drōme	airplane storage place.
airplane	âir′ plāne	heavier-than-air craft.
airport	âir′ pōrt	aircraft landing place.
altimeter	ăl tĭm′ ĕ tēr	altitude-measuring apparatus.
altitude	ăl′ tĭ tūde	height, position, or region.
ascend	ăs çĕnd′	take an upward direction.
atmosphere	ăt′ mŏs phēre	air surrounding the earth.
aviator	ā′ vĭ ā tŏr	operator of an airplane.
ballast	băl′ lȧst	anything that gives steadiness.
balloon	băl lōōn′	airtight bag filled with gas.
beacon	bēa′ eon	warning or guidance signal.
dirigible	dĭr′ ĭ ġĭ ble	cigar-shaped balloon.
gliding	glīd′ ĭng	flying without power.
hangar	hăŋg′ ãr	airplane housing shelter.
helicopter	hĕl ĭ eŏp′ tēr	having vertical rotating screws.
hydroplane	hȳ′ drŏ plāne	gliding motorboat.
monoplane	mŏn′ ŏ plāne	airplane with one set of wings.
parachute	păr′ ȧ çhųte (shōōt)	device for making a descent.
pilot	pī′ lŏt	licensed airplane flier.
propeller	prŏ pĕl′ lēr	propelling apparatus.
rudder	rŭd′ dēr	vertically controlling device.
spiral	spī′ răl	moving in a circle.

Refer to a dictionary for definition, pronunciation, and use of:

airway,   biplane,   cabin,   elevation,   navigator.

The United States Army, Navy, and Bureau of Standards officially adopted *airplane* as the standard spelling in preference to the early form, *aeroplane*, which is still used by British writers. Airplanes are classified as monoplanes, biplanes, triplanes, quadruplanes, or multiplanes, according to the number of parts into which their main supporting surface is divided.

The Radio

aerial	ā ē′ rĭ ăl	receiving or distributing wire.
amplifier	ăm′ plĭ fī ēr	volume-increasing apparatus.
antenna	ăn těn′ nà	wire on a receiving set for receiving radiating waves.
audibility	au dĭ bĭl′ ĭ tў	strength of sound impulses.
audition	au dĭ′ tion	public hearing.
battery	băt′ tēr ў	electric generating apparatus.
broadcast	brôad′ eăst	message or music over a radio.
detector	dĕ tĕe′ tŏr	wave-detecting device.
dial	dī′ ăl	movable disc with pointer.
frequency	frē′ quĕn çў	rate of vibrations per second.
grid leak	grĭd lēak	electron grid resistance.
interference	ĭn tēr fēr′ ĕnçe	confliction of electric waves.
kilocycle	kĭl′ ŏ çȳ ele	1000 cycles per second.
meter	mē′ tēr	measure of length.
oscillator	ŏs′ çĭl lā tŏr	radio-frequency generator.
radiogram	rā′ dĭ ŏ grăm	message sent by radio.
radiograph	rā′ dĭ ŏ grăph	X-ray photograph.
resonance	rĕş′ ŏ nănçe	vibrating quality of sound.
socket	sŏck′ ĕt	support for holding a tube.
static	stăt′ ĭe	atmospheric disturbance.
transformer	trăns fôrm′ ēr	device for converting energy.
transmitter	trăns mĭt′ tēr	message sending apparatus.
tuning	tūn′ ĭng	selecting proper wave length.
voltage	vōlt′ aġe (ĭj)	power expressed in volts.
wireless	wīre′ lĕss	without the use of wires.

Refer to a dictionary for definition, pronunciation, and use of:

ground,   selectivity,   vibration,   volts,   wave.

Antenna (plural *antennae*) is usually an elevated collecting wire or rod held in a vertical or horizontal position from a mast, tower, or the like. It may be called a *feeler* by means of which a radio set catches the waves. The word *antenna* is from the Greek and literally means "to feel." It is an organ of touch, or a feeler, attached in pairs to the head of an insect, or an animal. It is sometimes called "a cat's whiskers."

Geographical Words

arctic	äre′ tĭe	near the north pole; frigid.
climate	₵lī′ mate (mĭt)	local weather conditions.
continent	₵ŏn′ tĭ nĕnt	great mass or body of land.
desert	dĕ₷′ ẽrt	dry, barren body of land.
equator	ē̆ quā′ tõr	great circle of the earth.
erosion	ē̆ rō′ sion (zhŭn)	act or result of wearing away.
fossil	fŏs′ sĭl	petrified remains of a plant.
geography	ġē̆ ŏg′ rȧ phȳ	description of the earth.
glacier	glā′ ciẽr (shẽr)	moving field of snow or ice.
harbor	här′ bõr	protected body of water.
hemisphere	hĕm ĭ′ sphēre	one-half of the earth.
island	īs′ lănd	land surrounded by water.
isthmus	ĭs*th*′ mŭs	narrow neck of land.
latitude	lăt′ ĭ tūde	distance from the equator.
longitude	lŏn′ ġĭ tūde	distance east or west.
meridian	mĕ rĭd′ ĭ ăn	at or relating to midday.
minerals	mĭn′ ẽr ăl₷	earthy or inorganic matter.
mountainous	moun′ taĭn oŭs	abounding in mountains.
peninsula	pĕn ĭn′ sŭ lȧ	land nearly surrounded by water.
plateau	plă teau′ (tō′)	elevated plane; table-land.
prairie	prâ*i*′ rĭe	meadow; grassland.
southern	soŭth′ ẽrn	situated in the south.
territory	tĕr′ rĭ tō rȳ	region or district of land.
tributary	trĭb′ ũ tar ȳ (tĕr)	stream flowing into larger stream or lake.
weather	wĕath′ ẽr	state of the atmosphere.

Refer to a dictionary for definition, pronunciation, and use of:

geology,   ocean,   surface,   torrid,   valley.

Slang is often defined as "the language of thieves, beggars, or gypsies." It is sometimes the jargon of a particular calling or group of society, as the "lawyer's lingo," or the college student's pet phrases, as *apple-polishing*, *bone-up*, or *to be goofy*. The general use of slang is evidence of an impoverished vocabulary or mental laziness. However, some words considered slang at one time have become acceptable as correct English, as in the use of *mob*, *cab*, *canter*, and *hoax*.

Athletic Games and Sports

amateur	ăm à teûr′	not a professional player.
amusement	à mūşe′ mĕnt	pleasing entertainment; play.
athletic	ăth lĕt′ ĭe	strong and vigorous; active.
bowling	bōwl′ ĭng	game played with bowls.
challenge	chăl′ lĕnģe	invitation to contest.
champion	chăm′ pĭ ὸn	winner of a prize or contest.
competitive	eŏm pĕt′ ĭ tĭve	open to competition.
contest	eŏn tĕst′	contend with another person.
entertainment	ĕn tēr tāin′ mĕnt	that which interests or amuses.
exercise	ĕx′ ēr çĭşe	train or strengthen by use.
fatigue	fà tïgue′	weariness from exertion.
fumble	fŭm′ ble	handle or play awkwardly.
gymnasium	ģў̆m nā′ şĭ ŭm	place for athletic exercise.
pageant	păģ′ ĕant	elaborate show or display.
pastime	pàs′ tīme	amusement; sport; recreation.
pennant	pĕn′ nănt	small, long, narrow flag.
prize	prīze	something to be won; award.
recreation	rĕe rĕ ā′ tion	diversion; play.
spectacular	spĕe tăe′ ủ lăr	making an unusual display.
sportsman	spōrts′ măn	one engaged in outdoor sport.
stadium	stā′ dĭ ŭm	arena for athletic contests.
swimming	swĭm′ mĭng	act of moving in the water.
tournament	toųr′ nà mĕnt	series of contests in skill.
trophy	trō′ phў̆	evidence of a victory.
umpire	ŭm′ pīre	referee; judge; arbitrator.

Refer to a dictionary for definition, pronunciation, and use of:

arena, athlete, intramural, pleasure, victory.

The Coloseum was a name applied to a Roman amphitheater built about 80 A.D. and in great part still standing giving mute evidence of the purpose for which it was erected. In modern usage the word is commonly spelled *coliseum* and refers to a theater, music hall, or a large building in which athletic sports may be held. The more common word for this latter purpose is *stadium*.

Athletic Games and Sports

LESSON 87	LESSON 88	LESSON 89
archery	fishing	physical
arena	fore	pitcher
assist	foul	players
award	foursome	quoits
balk	goal	racket
baseman	golf	referee
batsman	gridiron	score
batting	grounder	scrimmage
bleachers	handicap	serve
boating	hazard	single
bunkers	hiking	skating
caddies	hockey	soccer
canoeing	holiday	spectators
captain	huddle	sports
catcher	hunting	strike
center	hurdle	substitute
checkers	inning	tackle
coach	liner	target
croquet	linesman	team
curve	links	tennis
diamond	mask	triple
double	match	vacation
dribble	muff	whitewash
error	muscular	winner
fielder	penalty	wrestling

Refer to a dictionary for definition, pronunciation, and use of:

badminton,   camping,   chess,   intercollegiate,   skiing.

Olympian pertains to a dweller on Olympus, a mountain in Macedonia. The Olympian games date back to 770 B.C. They were held every four years in honor of the god Zeus. The games were of the usual athletic type. The prize of the victor consisted of a crown of wild olives, a palm branch, and the right to erect a statue in the Altis or sacred precinct. A modified form of the Olympian games, consisting of international athletic events and races, is held once in four years; the first was held in Athens in 1896.

89

Homonyms: Words Identical in Sound but Differing in Meaning

LESSON 90

ceiling, overhead.
sealing, close hermetically.

cellar, underground room.
seller, merchant.

cite, quote.
sight, ability to see.
site, plot of ground.

dew, condensed vapor.
due, debt; something owed.

grate, framework of bars.
great, grand; very large.

grocer, dealer in provisions.
grosser, coarser.

knead, mix; work.
need, necessity.

medal, commemorative reward.
meddle, interfere.

metal, refined ore.
mettle, courage; ardor.

mustard, plant with pungent taste.
mustered, summoned together.

ode, lyric poem.
owed, debt due.

peace, absence of war.
piece, small portion.

LESSON 91

pedal, foot lever.
peddle, to sell.

plait, braid or interweave.
plate, serving dish.

praise, laud or commend.
prays, implores; petitions.
preys, plunders.

right, correct.
rite, ceremony.
wright, workman.
write, form letters.

ring, circular object.
wring, squeeze hard.

soar, fly.
sore, painful.

succor, relief or help.
sucker, fish.

stake, piece of wood.
steak, cut of meat.

throne, royal seat.
thrown, cast a distance.

wade, walk in water.
weighed, tested.

wait, stay or remain.
weight, heavy mass.

Refer to a dictionary for definition, pronunciation, and use of:
quarts, quartz;   suite, sweet;   throe, throw;   wrung, rung.

A desirable plan for determining the proper use of homonyms is to form sentences illustrating their usage. Illustrate in sentences so as to show the difference in meaning of: *cereal, serial; buy, by; wrapping, rapping; minor, miner; new, knew.*

Ward is an English suffix denoting "toward," as *forward, backward, upward, downward, inward, outward,* and *homeward.* Compile an additional list of similar words.

Homonyms: Words Identical in Sound but Differing in Meaning

allowed, permitted.
aloud, so as to be heard.

altar, communion table.
alter, change or modify.

bald, without hair.
bawled, cried aloud.

baron, title.
barren, unproductive.

beach, sandy shore.
beech, tree of hard wood.

berry, small fruit.
bury, cover over.

bolder, more fearless.
boulder, large, round rock.

bridal, relating to marriage.
bridle, head harness.

calendar, almanac.
calender, pressing machine.

canvas, strong cloth.
canvass, solicit.

carat, weight.
caret, mark.
carrot, vegetable.

sole, bottom of a shoe.
soul, spirit.

berth, place to sleep.
birth, act of being born.

cannon, large gun.
canon, law or rule.

cereal, grain.
serial, related sequence.

cession, withdrawal.
session, meeting.

colonel, army officer.
kernel, single seed.

core, inner part.
corps, body of troops.

currant, small fruit.
current, flow of water.

fair, just or equitable.
fare, passage-money.

foul, filthy or vile.
fowl, any large bird.

heal, make well.
heel, part of the foot.

hear, listen to.
here, at this place.

vain, conceited.
vane, wind indicator.
vein, blood vessel.

Refer to a dictionary for definition, pronunciation, and use of:

acclamation, acclimation; eyelet, islet; scene, seen; tax, tacks.

Exercise care in pronunciation. N *w, due, use* have the same sound as heard in *few.* Practice pronouncing *educate, figure, picture, suit, suite, produce, Tuesday, duly, nuisance* until you can do so readily and correctly.

Use a dictionary in which the definitions are sufficiently comprehensive to give a correct interpretation. A student read a sentence in class to illustrate the word *erroneous.* He said, "My grandfather has erroneous teeth." His dictionary defined this word with only one meaning, "false."

Homonyms: Words Identical in Sound but Differing in Meaning

LESSON 94

dire, distressful; terrible.
dyer, one who colors.
dual, double; two-fold.
duel, fight to kill.
dyeing, coloring.
dying, expiring.
felloe, wheel rim.
fellow, person; associate.
flour, ground meal.
flower, blossom.
freeze, congeal.
frieze, coarse cloth.
gamble, play for stakes.
gambol, play or frolic.
grater, instrument.
greater, larger than.
groan, moan.
grown, increased in size.
guessed, supposed that.
guest, visitor.
him, personal pronoun.
hymn, sacred song.
idle, lazy.
idol, image.
idyl, short poem.

LESSON 95

cent, small coin.
scent, odor; fragrance.
sent, dispatched.
chased, pursued.
chaste, pure.
higher, taller than.
hire, employ.
holy, sacred; pure in heart.
wholly, completely.
hoarse, harsh; husky.
horse, equine animal.
indict, accuse.
indite, write.
lean, not fat.
lien, legal claim.
leased, rented.
least, smallest.
lessen, make smaller.
lesson, instructions.
pair, two.
pare, remove outer part.
pear, fruit.
road, highway.
rode, did ride.
rowed, propelled a boat.

Refer to a dictionary for definition, pronunciation, and use of:

nun, none; peer, pier; pause, paws; sail, sale; troop, troup.

The value of a comma. The state legislature of North Dakota enacted a law in 1929 making it illegal to sleep in a hotel. "No hotel, restaurant, dining room or kitchen shall be used as a sleeping or dressing room by an employee or other persons." Remove the comma after the word hotel and the effect of the law is changed. A legislative amendment would be necessary to make such a correction.

Words with Two Pronunciations[1]

collect	eŏl′ lĕet	certain short prayer.
	eŏl lĕet′	ask and receive payment.
compress	eŏm′ prĕss	in surgery, a soft pad.
	eŏm prĕss′	condense, squeeze together.
confine	eŏn′ fīne	inclosure; boundary.
	eŏn fīne′	restrain by a barrier.
content	eŏn′ tĕnt	arrangement of topics.
	eŏn tĕnt′	be satisfied with conditions.
contrast	eŏn′ trăst	differences in appearance.
	eŏn trăst′	compare differences.
digest	dī′ ġĕst	classified body of information.
	dĭ ġĕst′	dissolve in the stomach.
ferment	fẽr′ mĕnt	state of agitation.
	fẽr mĕnt′	undergo a change.
gallant	găl′ lănt	gay, fashionable person.
	găl lănt′	act as an escort to a lady.
minute	mĭn′ ute (ĭt)	sixty seconds.
	mĭ nūte′	wee; very small.
permit	pẽr′ mĭt	written or printed pass.
	pẽr mĭt′	consent; allow; authorize.
produce	prŏd′ ūçe	agricultural or farm products.
	prŏ dūçe′	create; make; originate.
purport	pûr′ pōrt	gist or tenor of the matter.
	pûr pōrt′	imply; convey.
rebel	rĕb′ ĕl	one in open opposition.
	rĕ bĕl′	resist authority.
record	rĕe′ ōrd	written entry.
	rĕ eôrd′	set down in writing.
refuse	rĕf′ ūṣe	worthless and waste material.
	rĕ fūṣe′	decline what is offered.
reprint	rē′ prĭnt	new or additional printing.
	rē prĭnt′	make additional copies.
torment	tôr′ mĕnt	something that causes suffering.
	tôr mĕnt′	worry; annoy; tease.

---

[1]*Explanation.* There are a number of words that undergo a change in meaning when the accent is changed. Ordinarily, nouns are accented on the first syllable, and verbs and adjectives on the second syllable. The foregoing list of words subject to a changed meaning when the accent is changed is not a complete list; it is merely suggestive.

Words Having Similar Sounds but Different Meanings

accept	ăe çĕpt′	take when offered; agree to.
except	ĕx çĕpt′	reject; omit or leave out.
adherence	ăd hēr′ ĕnçe	attachment; holding firmly.
adherents	ăd hēr′ ĕnts	supporters of a policy.
ascent	ăs cĕnt′	upward slope or movement.
assent	ăs sĕnt′	agreement or concurrence.
assistance	ăs sĭst′ ănçe	help; aid; succor; support.
assistants	ăs sĭst′ ănts	those who give help or aid.
attendance	ăt tĕnd′ ănçe	number of persons present.
attendants	ăt tĕnd′ ănts	those who serve or follow.
affect	ăf fĕet′	make pretense; influence.
effect	ĕf fĕet′	bring about or accomplish.
commence	eŏm mĕnçe′	start; take a first step.
comments	eŏm′ mĕnts	expression of an opinion.
confidant	eŏn fĭ dȧnt′	one trusted with a secret.
confident	eon′ fĭ dĕnt	sure; feeling certain.
decease	dĕ çēase′	cease to live; death.
disease	dĭṣ ēaṣe′	illness or physical disorder.
deprecate	dĕp′ rĕ eāte	express strong disapproval of.
depreciate	dĕ prē′ ci āte (shĭ)	lessen in value.
deference	dĕf′ ĕr ĕnçe	respect for another's opinion.
difference	dĭf′ fēr ĕnçe	disagreement; distinction.
populace	pŏp′ ŭ lace (lĭs)	common people collectively.
populous	pŏp′ ŭ loŭs	containing many inhabitants.
Populus	Pŏp′ ŭ lŭs	belonging to the poplar tree.

Refer to a dictionary for definition, pronunciation, and use of:

personal, personnel, respectably, respectively, respectfully.

Sirloin (from *sur*, meaning above) has been changed in spelling to sirloin, as if from "sir." There is an absurd and make-believe story of how an English king once knighted a loin of beef in enthusiastic appreciation of his national dish, and it thus became a Sir-loin.

Words Having Similar Sounds but Different Meanings

eminent	ĕm′ ĭ nĕnt	prominent; distinguished.
imminent	ĭm′ mĭ nĕnt	full of danger; threatening.
elusion	ĕ lū′ sion (zhŭn)	clever act of evasion.
illusion	ĭl lū′ sion (zhŭn)	false appearance; trick.
eruption	ĕ rŭp′ tion	breaking out; bursting forth.
irruption	ĭr rŭp′ tion	breaking in upon suddenly.
incite	ĭn çīte′	arouse or stir; move to action.
insight	ĭn′ sīght	clear understanding.
ingenious	ĭn gēn′ ious (yŭs)	having inventive ability.
ingenuous	ĭn gĕn′ ū oŭs	frank; artless; sincere.
palate	păl′ ate (ĭt)	roof of the mouth.
palette	păl′ ĕtte	painter's color board.
pallet	păl′ lĕt	small and mean bed.
plaintiff	plāin′ tĭff	one who begins a lawsuit.
plaintive	plāin′ tĭve	expressing sorrow; mournful.
practicable	prăc′ tĭ cả ble	feasible.
practical	prăc′ tĭ căl	useful, not theoretical.
presence	prĕs′ ĕnçe	nearness; act of being near.
presents	prĕs′ ĕnts	gifts; donations.
profit	prŏf′ ĭt	increase over cost.
prophet	prŏph′ ĕt	one who foretells events.
reference	rĕf′ ẽr ĕnçe	quoted passage; testimonial.
reverence	rĕv′ ẽr ĕnçe	fear mingled with respect.
residence	rĕṣ′ ĭ dĕnçe	home where one lives.
residents	rĕṣ′ ĭ dĕnts	inhabitants; population.

Refer to a dictionary for definition, pronunciation, and use of:

bread,   bred,   statute,   stature,   statue.

Illegal Acts: Is it illegal to melt coins or destroy, by burning, paper money? It is not illegal to do so, but it is illegal to attempt to pass mutilated coins or paper money. The government would gain by the destruction of paper money as these notes could not be presented for redemption.

Synonyms Derived from Different Languages

Greek	Latin	Anglo-Saxon
LESSON 99	LESSON 100	LESSON 101
agony	suffering	pain
analogy	similarity	likeness
antagonist	opponent	foe
antipathy	repugnance	hatred
archaic	antique	old
catalog	inventory	list
cauterize	corrode	burn
character	reputation	name
charitable	beneficent	kind
economical	frugal	sparing
emphasis	accent	stress
energy	force	strength
irony	satire	wit
laconic	concise	short
method	order	way
mimic	imitate	ape
monarch	emperor	king
pathetic	distressful	sad
pedagogue	instructor	teacher
politic	expedient	wise
scholar	student	learner
scope	view	aim
sketch	picture	outline
synonymous	similar	alike
tomb	sepulcher	grave

Refer to a dictionary for definition, pronunciation, and use of:
assistance, commence, cycle, liberty, velocity.

Synonyms are commonly defined in the dictionaries as words in the language "having the same or nearly the same essential meaning." However, there is no such thing as a word having the same meaning as another word. Having several words to represent nearly the same meaning prevents useless repetition and encourages the use of words to give the most delicate shade of meaning. As a person becomes educated he uses words with greater nicety and distinction of meaning giving evidence of an extensive and valuable vocabulary.

Words Frequently Mispronounced

acumen	ă eū′ měn	keenness of insight.
altercation	ạl tẽr eā′ tion	dispute carried on with anger.
construe	eŏn strụe′	make plain; interpret.
contour	eŏn′ toụr	outline of a body or figure.
contrary	eŏn′ tra rў (trĕr)	in an opposite manner.
definite	dĕf′ ĭ nĭt*e*	having certain fixed limits.
dishevel	dĭ shĕv′ ĕl	disarrange, as the hair.
extant	ĕx′ tănt	still living; not out of use.
extol	ĕx tŏl′	praise or laud highly.
garrulous	găr′ rụ loŭs	talkative about trivial things.
grimace	grĭ māç*e*′	twist or distort the face.
hospitable	hŏs′ pĭ tȧ bl*e*	showing kindness to guests.
implacable	ĭm plā′ eȧ bl*e*	unappeasable.
irremediable	ĭr rẽ mē′ dĭ ȧ bl*e*	incurable.
jugular	jŭg′ ụ lär	large vein of the neck.
larynx	lăr′ ynx (ўŋks)	upper part of the windpipe.
memento	mẽ měn′ tō	souvenir or reminder.
memorable	měm′ ŏ rȧ bl*e*	worthy of being remembered.
menial	mē′ nĭ ăl	work of a servant.
misconstrue	mĭs eŏn strụe′	misinterpret.
obituary	ŏ bĭt′ụ ar ў (ĕr)	notice of a person's death.
obligatory	ŏb lĭg′ ȧ tō rў	legally or morally binding.
sentimental	sĕn tĭ měn′ tăl	appealing to the feelings.
status	stā′ tŭs	fixed or legal standing.
vagary	vȧ gâr′ ў	departure from normal or logical order.

Refer to a dictionary for definition, pronunciation, and use of:

corpulence, diagonal, dining, massacre, microscopic.

A diacritical mark is a mark used to indicate the different sounds of letters, and to indicate the pronunciation of words. Since the same letter must sometimes be used to represent several different sounds, diacritical marks have been adopted to distinguish the particular sound of the letter. The letter *a*, for instance, has eight different sounds. Each sound is indicated by a special mark and each mark has a different name.

LESSON 103

Words Commonly Mispronounced

authority	au thŏr′ ĭ tỹ	power to compel obedience.
command	eŏm mȧnd′	direct with authority.
conscientious	eŏn sci en′ tious (shĭ ĕn shŭs)	acting uprightly; faithful.
courier	eo̤ur′ ĭ ēr	messenger or attendant.
courteous	eoûr′ tĕ o̤ŭs	polite; civil; gracious.
direct	dĭ rĕet′	show the way; straightforward.
duplicate	dū′ plĭ eȧte	exact copy; second copy.
finance	fĭ nănçe′	art of managing money.
gallantry	găl′ lănt rỹ	attentiveness to women.
gallery	găl′ lēr ỹ	long narrow room or hall.
heroine	hĕr′ ṏ ĭne	woman of courage.
hideous	hĭd′ ĕ o̤ŭs	horribly ugly; frightful.
idea	ī dē′ ȧ	image in the mind; thought.
menagerie	mĕ năġ′ ēr ĭe	collection of wild animals.
pathos	pā′ thŏs	that which arouses emotions.
perhaps	pēr hăps′	possibly but not certainly.
perspiration	pēr spĭ rā′ tion	excretion through the pores.
realistic	rē ăl ĭs′ tĭe	lifelike; things as they are.
reptile	rĕp′ tĭle	crawling animal; base person.
resonant	rĕẓ′ ṏ nănt	resounding or echoing back.
saucy	sa̤u′ çỹ	pert; impudent; insolent.
saunter	sa̤un′ tēr	walk about slowly and idly.
serious	sē′ rĭ o̤ŭs	solemn, not trifling; earnest.
thwart	thwa̧rt	oppose, obstruct, or block.
wand	wa̧nd	small rod; staff of authority.

Refer to a dictionary for definition, pronunciation, and use of:

against,   daughter,   horizon,   immersion,   inference.

Syllabication is the act or method of dividing words into syllables. A word consists of one or more syllables. A word is a succession of syllables, as each syllable is a succession of letters. Long words may be pronounced readily by pronouncing the syllables. A knowledge of syllabication is helpful in correct pronunciation, and correct pronunciation is an aid in correct spelling.

There is no *a* in the word *shepherd.* Contrast this word with *sheep, herd, herdsman.*

98

Tendency to Mispronounce Certain Syllables

bachelor	băch′ ĕ lŏr	man who has not married.
basin	bā′ s*i*n	shallow circular vessel.
bouquet	bou quet′(boo kā′)	bunch of flowers; nosegay.
destroy	dĕ stroy′	put an end to; demolish.
dexterous	dĕx′ tĕr o*u*s	clever; expert; adroit; quick.
different	dĭf′ fĕr ĕnt	unlike; diversified.
duteous	dū′ tĕ o*u*s	obedient; showing respect.
eclectic	ĕe lĕe′ t*i*e	picking from many sources.
erroneous	ĕr rō′ nĕ o*u*s	containing an error; mistaken.
fragile	frăg′ ĭl*e*	easily broken; very delicate.
governor	gòv′ ẽr nŏr	chief executive of a state.
impious	ĭm′ pĭ o*u*s	wicked; irreverent; profane.
importance	ĭm pôr′ tănç*e*	having much significance.
infamous	ĭn′ fȧ mo*u*s	of very bad reputation.
majesty	măj′ ĕs tў	exalted dignity; grandeur.
manners	măn′ nẽr$	conduct or deportment.
model	mŏd′ *e*l	exact small copy; sample.
oblique	ŏb lique′ (lēk′)	slanting, not upright.
perpetrate	pẽr′ pĕ trāt*e*	carry through; commit.
regular	rĕg′ ŭ lȧr	done in the proper way.
sailor	sā*i*l′ ŏr	common seaman; mariner.
several	sĕv′ ẽr ăl	more than two, but not many.
standard	stănd′ ȧrd	accepted or established rule.
superfluous	sŭ pẽr′ flu̧ o*u*s	more than enough; useless.
various	vâr′ ĭ o*u*s	several or many; different.

Refer to a dictionary for definition, pronunciation, and use of:

accommodate, directorate, enigma, factor, ritual.

Syllabication. A syllable contains one or more vowels. A vowel is a letter that can be sounded by itself; as *a, e, i, o, u*, sometimes *y*, and *w*. A word with only one vowel cannot have more than one syllable. The letters A, I, and O are the only letters that form words in themselves.

A *syllable* is the unit of a word, and it is not divisible. Words are divisible between syllables only. A word of one syllable is a monosyllable, as *few*; of two syllables, a dissyllable, as *window*; of three syllables, a trisyllable, as *history*.

Words Containing Silent Consonants

asthma	ăşth′ mà	chronic breathing disease.
attack	ăt tăck′	assail, as with weapons.
calmly	eälm′ lў	in a quiet manner.
condemn	eŏn dĕm*n*′	censure; denounce; curse.
cudgel	eŭ*dġ*′ ĕl	short heavy club or stick.
dough	dō*ugh*	unbaked bread.
drawl	dr*ạ*wl	long drawn-out sound.
exhaust	ĕx̱ *h*ạust′	use up completely; wear out.
extraordinary	ĕx traôr′ dĭ nar ў (nĕr)	unusual; uncommon.
fighting	fī*gh*t′ ĭng	pertaining to a conflict.
gnash	*g*năsh	snap the teeth together.
grudge	grŭ*dġe*	give unwillingly.
hasten	hās′ te*n*	be in a hurry; go quickly.
initials	ĭn ĭ′ tials (shăl̦ş)	first letters of a name.
knack	*k*năck	skill; facility; dexterity.
listen	lĭs′ te*n*	hear; hearken; eavesdrop.
notch	nŏ*t*ch	cut a v-shaped mark.
nudge	nŭ*dġe*	gentle push with the elbows.
ridge	rĭ*dġe*	upper edge of a roof; elevation.
scythe	scȳ*the*	curved blade for mowing.
sigh	sī*gh*	long, deep, audible breath.
stomach	stŏm′ ăe*h*	organ of digestion.
straight	strā*igh*t	having but one direction.
thorough	thôr′ ŏ*ugh*	finished; not superficial.
wretch	*w*rĕtch	miserable pitiable creature.

Refer to a dictionary for definition, pronunciation, and use of:

balm,   **bustle,**   **fleck,**   **robust,**   **wharf.**

Syllabication. A knowledge of syllabication is valuable in knowing how words should be divided at the end of a line. At the end of a line the word should be separated between syllables.

A combination of vowels or consonants pronounced as a single letter should not be divided. Such combinations are illustrated by *ai*, ea, *eau*, *gh*, *ph*, *str*, *tch*, and many others.

To be conscious that you are ignorant is a great way to knowledge.

—DISRAELI.

Words Containing Silent Consonants

abridgment	à brĭ*dg*′ mĕnt	shortened form; abstract.
acknowledge	ăe *k*nŏ*wl*′ ĕd*g*e	admit to be true; concede.
although	ạl th̄ōu*gh*′	notwithstanding; even if.
awful	ạ*w*′ fụl	dreadful or appalling.
awkward	ạ*w*k′ wärd	lacking in skill or grace.
bough	bou*gh*	limb of a tree; offshoot.
bought	bôu*gh*t	purchased.
climbing	elīm*b*′ ĭng	ascending with difficulty.
doubtful	dou*b*t′ fụl	uncertain.
gnaw	*g*nạ*w*	bite so as to wear away.
honest	*h*ŏn′ ĕst	free from fraud or deceit.
knowledge	*k*nŏ*wl*′ ĕd*g*e	information; learning; skill.
lack	lăck	be without; be deficient.
malign	mà lī*g*n′	malicious; hateful; evil.
naughty	nau*gh*′ tў	mischievous; misbehaving.
night	nī*gh*t	time between dusk and dawn.
rhythm	r*h*ў*th*m	regularity of occurrence.
scenery	scēn′ ẽr ў	stage representation.
smack	smăck	quick, sharp noise; slap.
stitch	stĭ*t*ch	acute pain in the side.
wholesome	*w*hōle′ sòm*e*	sound mind, body, or morals.
wrangle	*w*răŋ′ gl*e*	dispute noisily or angrily.
wrapper	*w*răp′ pẽr	outer covering; loose gown.
wrathful	*w*ràth′ fụl	furious; extremely angry.
yolk	yō*l*k	yellow part of an egg.

Refer to a dictionary for definition, pronunciation, and use of:

diphthong,   mown,   wreathe,   wrest,   writhe.

Syllabication. The dividing hyphen should be at the end of the line and not at the beginning of the next line.

It is not desirable to divide proper names at the end of a line.

One letter should not stand alone at the end of a line or at the beginning of a line. It is desirable that at least two letters should end the line and three letters begin the next line.

Divide a word so that the part before the hyphen will suggest the whole word.

Avoid excessive syllabication.

Words Containing ei and ie

aggrieve	ăg grĭēve′	cause sorrow, pain, or injury.
audience	au′ dĭ ĕnçe	body of hearers.
belief	bĕ lĭēf′	faith; creed; conviction.
brevier	brĕ vĭēr′	small size of type.
briefly	brĭēf′ lў	in a few words; concisely.
conceive	₵ŏn çēive′	originate or form a thought.
deceit	dĕ çēit′	double dealing; lie; fraud.
eighty	ₑight′ ў	four times twenty; fourscore.
fierce	fĭērçe	ferocious; vehement; fiery.
friendly	frĭĕnd′ lў	not hostile; kindly disposed.
grievous	grĭēv′ oŭs	hard to bear; burdensome.
hosier	hō′ sier (zhĕr)	dealer in stockings.
inalienable	ĭn āl′ien à ble (yĕn)	incapable of being transferred.
incipient	ĭn çĭp′ ĭ ĕnt	beginning to appear or exist.
inveigle	ĭn vēi′gle	lead astray by deception.
leisure	lēi′ sure (zhĕr)	freedom from work or worry.
neighbor	nₑigh′ bŏr	one who lives close by.
outweigh	out wₑigh′	exceed in weight.
patience	pā′ tience (shĕns)	willing to wait; fortitude.
perceive	pĕr çēive′	see, feel, hear, or understand.
receive	rĕ çēive′	come into possession of.
recipient	rĕ çĭp′ ĭ ĕnt	one who receives a gift.
reigning	rₑign′ ĭng	exercising power or authority.
relief	rĕ lĭēf′	aid; relaxation; comfort.
retrieve	rĕ trĭēve′	gain back, recover, or save.

Refer to a dictionary for definition, pronunciation, and use of:

beige,   either,   heiress,   neither,   surfeit.

There are several rules for the use of *ei* and *ie*, and several exceptions to the rules. For instance: in words spelled with *ei* or *ie* (pronounced *ee*) *e* follows *c*, and *i* follows all other letters. Thus:

Put *i* before *e* except after *c*,
Or when sounded like *a*, as in neighbor and neigh;
And except seize, and seizure, and also leisure,
Forfeit, weird, height, either and neither.

Words Containing ei or ie

achieve à chiēve′ accomplish successfully; win.
acquiesce ăc quĭ ĕsçe′ consent without objecting.
alien āl′ ien (yĕn) belonging to another country.
chief chiēf principal person or thing.
deign deign condescend; esteem worthy.
feign feign pretend; not real or genuine.
field fiēld inclosed, cultivated ground.
forfeit fôr′ feĭt loss by fine or penalty.
frontier frón tiēr′ border line of a country.
inconvenience ĭn cŏn vēn′ ience annoyance or embarrassment.
　　　　　　(yĕns)
inveigh ĭn veigh′ attack with harsh criticism.
lenient lē′ nĭ ĕnt merciful, mild; not severe.
niece niēçe daughter of brother or sister.
patient pā′ tient (shĕnt) calmly bearing suffering.
relieve rĕ liēve′ give comfort or aid; lighten.
reprieve rĕ priēve′ delay or postpone punishment.
review rĕ view′ (vū) examine with great care.
shield shiēld cover from danger; protect.
shriek shriēk sharp shrill outcry.
sleight sleīght (slīt) artful or dexterous trick.
species spē′ cies (shĭz) variety; kind; group.
their their belonging to them.
tierce tiērçe cask of forty-two gallons.
veil veil cover; mask; pretense.
yield yiēld give up; give in return.

Refer to a dictionary for definition, pronunciation, and use of:

adieu,　　　**lieu,**　　　**mien,**　　　**seizure,**　　　**tier.**

Words in which the diphthongs *ei* or *ie* occur are a source of grief in many instances in determining the correct spelling. There is a general rule (with exceptions, of course) that *ei* follows after *c* and *ie* follows after *l*, and a number of other consonants.

One of the common rules is expressed thus: The word *Celia* may often be used as a key. Thus, *c* is followed by *e* and *l* by *i*; as, *receive* and *believe*.

Words Containing ei or ie

believe	bĕ l*ie*ve'	have faith or confidence.
conceit	cŏn çē*it'*	high opinion of one's self.
convenience	cŏn vēn' i*e*nçe (yĕns)	that which promotes comfort.
deceitful	dĕ çē*it'* ful	not dependable; insincere.
deficient	dĕ fĭ' ci*e*nt (shĕnt)	lacking in something necessary.
eighth	e*igh*th	next in order after seven.
fiend	f*ie*nd	one who is wickedly cruel.
foreign	fŏr' e*ig*n	belonging elsewhere.
freight	fre*igh*t	goods moved by a carrier.
grief	gr*ie*f	mental distress; sorrow.
grievance	gr*ie*v' ănçe	cause of annoyance; injury.
grieve	gr*ie*ve	feel grief or sorrow.
heir	h*ei*r	one who inherits property.
mischief	mĭs' chĭef	trouble or vexation caused by human agency.
neigh	ne*igh*	cry of a horse; whinny.
pierce	p*ie*rçe	make a hole through.
priest	pr*ie*st	pastor; minister; clergyman.
proficient	prō fĭ' cient (shĕnt)	well-skilled; adept.
rein	re*i*n	restrain; control; manage.
scientific	scī ĕn tĭf' ĭc	according to prescribed rules.
seize	se*i*ze	take possession by force.
sieve	s*ie*ve	straining utensil.
thief	th*ie*f	one who robs or steals.
weird	we*i*rd	unearthly; supernatural.
wield	w*ie*ld	handle or manage; use freely.

Refer to a dictionary for definition, pronunciation, and use of:

bier,   **height,**   **liege,**   **reverie,**   **skein.**

One of the rules for the use of *ei* and *ie* is thus expressed:

When the letter *c* you spy, put the *e* before the *i*.
If you do not spy a *c* place the *i* before the *e*,
But either, neither, leisure, siege, are four exceptions if you please.

104

The Suffixes ence, ance, and ense

absence	ăb′ sĕnçe	state of being away.
alliance	ăl lī′ ănçe	league between nations.
annoyance	ăn noy′ ănçe	cause of trouble; vexation.
competence	eŏm′ pĕ tĕnçe	fitness; capability; ability.
confidence	eŏn′ fĭ dĕnçe	trust in one's self or others.
dependence	dĕ pĕnd′ ĕnçe	that on which one relies.
distance	dĭs′ tănçe	space between two objects.
endurance	ĕn dūr′ ănçe	fortitude; continuance.
excellence	ĕx′ çĕl lĕnçe	superior virtue; high merit.
experience	ĕx pē′ rĭ ĕnçe	knowledge gained by practice.
hindrance	hĭn′ drănçe	obstruction; that which stops.
impertinence	ĭm pĕr′ tĭ nĕnçe	rudeness; impudence.
impudence	ĭm′ pū dĕnçe	sauciness; disrespect.
influence	ĭn′ flu ĕnçe	power to attract or sway.
insolence	ĭn′ sŏ lĕnçe	rudeness; overbearing conduct.
nonsense	nŏn′ sĕnse	words or action without sense.
obedience	ŏ bē′ dĭ ĕnçe	willingness to obey.
occurrence	ŏe eûr′ rĕnçe	that which happens; event.
performance	pĕr fôrm′ ănçe	act of achieving; feat; deed.
persistence	pĕr sĭst′ ĕnçe	endurance; staying qualities.
reliance	rĕ lī′ ănçe	trust; confidence.
resemblance	rĕ ṣĕm′ blănçe	likeness in any way; similarity.
resistance	rĕ ṣĭst′ ănçe	opposition; striving against.
significance	sĭg nĭf′ ĭ eănçe	meaning.
violence	vī′ ŏ lĕnçe	use of strength or force.

Refer to a dictionary for definition, pronunciation, and use of:

abstinence, contrivance, impatience, lenience, reluctance.

There are only a few words ending in the suffix *ense.* Of all the words that end thus, all but two of them—*nonsense* and *incense*—are accented on the last syllable; as *immense, expense.*

The suffixes *ance* and *ence* denote action, process, quality, or state; as *assistance, brilliance.*

The word *maintenance* is derived from *maintain.* Note the material difference in the spelling of the two words.

Suffixes *ize*, *ise*, and *yze*

advertise	ăd′ vẽr tīẓe	give publicity; announce.
analyze	ăn′ à lȳze	separate a thing into parts and examine critically.
antagonize	ăn tăg′ ŏ nīze	show opposition or hostility.
authorize	au′ thõr īze	give authority; empower.
capsize	căp sīze′	upset or overturn a boat.
catechize	căt′ ĕ ₵hīze	question systematically.
chastise	chăs tīẓe′	correct by bodily punishment.
civilize	₵ĭv′ ĭ līze	reclaim from savage life.
criticize	₵rĭt′ ĭ ₵īze	find fault; express judgment.
despise	dĕ spīẓe′	look upon with contempt.
devise	dĕ vīẓe′	plan; form in the mind; scheme.
disguise	dĭs gu̇īẓe′	change the appearance.
equalize	ē′ quăl īze	make equal or uniform.
hypnotize	hy̆p′ nŏ tīze	produce artificial sleep.
itemize	ī′ tĕm īze	set forth by items.
naturalize	năt′ u̞ răl īze	give the rights of citizenship.
paralyze	păr′ à lȳze	render powerless; disable.
patronize	pāt′ rȯn īze	trade with customarily.
pulverize	pŭl′ vẽr īze	reduce to powder or dust.
realize	rē′ ăl īze	know from experience.
revise	rĕ vīẓe′	make changes or corrections.
scrutinize	serū′ tĭ nīze	examine very closely.
subsidize	sŭbsĭ dīze	aid a private enterprise with public money.
sympathize	sy̆m′ pà thīze	feel pity for another person.
utilize	ū′ tĭ līze	put in use; turn to account.

Refer to a dictionary for definition, pronunciation, and use of:

comprise, demise, improvise, systematize, temporize.

The suffixes *ise*, *ize*, and *yze* are used to denote equality, condition, or being. *Analyze* and *paralyze* are the only words that end in the suffix *yze*. The most commonly used suffix in all other words is *ize*. Many of the words that end in *ise* are usually sounded as though they were spelled with *ize*. There is a tendency to increase the use of *ize*.

Suffixes ize, ise, and yze

agonize	ăg′ ŏ nīze	suffer great pain or anguish.
apologize	ă pŏl′ ŏ ġīze	express an excuse or regret.
appetizer	ăp′ pĕ tīz ẽr	food that whets the appetite.
apprise	ăp prīze′	give notice; inform.
arise	à rīze′	get up; come into action.
baptize	băp tīze′	dip or immerse in water.
brutalize	brụ′ tăl īze	make beastly or inhuman.
demoralize	dĕ mŏr′ ăl īze	corrupt in morals; disorganize.
emphasize	ĕm′ phà sīze	force; lay stress upon.
enfranchise	ĕn frăn′ chīze	grant one the right to vote.
eulogize	eū′ lŏ ġīze	praise highly; extol.
generalize	ġĕn′ ẽr ăl īze	treat in an ordinary way.
harmonize	här′ mŏn īze	cause to agree; reconcile.
jeopardize	jĕop′ ãrd īze	expose to loss or danger.
legalize	lē′ găl īze	make legal; authorize.
modernize	mŏd′ ẽrn īze	make or become modern.
ostracize	ŏs′ trà çīze	banish from society.
otherwise	ŏth′ ẽr wīze	under other circumstances.
recognize	rĕe′ ŏg nīze	admit knowledge of; know again.
specialize	spĕ′ cial īze (shăl)	make specific or individual.
standardize	stănd′ àrd īze	reduce to an established rule.
stigmatize	stĭg′ mà tīze	hold up to shame or infamy.
surmise	sûr mīze′	guess or conjecture based on slight evidence.
surprise	sur prīze′ (sẽr)	unexpected; taken unawares.
visualize	vĭẓ′ ụ ăl īze	form a mental picture.

Refer to a dictionary for definition, pronunciation, and use of:

deputize,   localize,   neutralize,   solemnize,   symbolize.

The suffix *ize* is commonly used when the word is derived from some other word. When it is not so derived, the ending is ordinarily *ise*.

"If you wish to *succeed* in learning to spell,
Proceed to *exceed* even those who do well."

The Suffixes able and ible

acceptable	ăe çĕpt′ à blе	worth receiving; agreeable.
accessible	ăe çĕs′ sĭ blе	easy of access or approach.
adaptable	à dăpt′ à blе	quality of being suitable.
debatable	dĕ bāt′ à blе	controversial.
definable	dĕ fīn′ à blе	explainable.
deniable	dĕ nī′ à blе	disputable.
despicable	dĕs′ pĭ eà blе	contemptible.
enviable	ĕn′ vĭ à blе	awakening a desire to possess.
excitable	ĕx çīt′ à blе	capable of being stirred up.
fallible	făl′ lĭ blе	liable to error or mistake.
inestimable	ĭn ĕs′ tĭ mà blе	above or beyond all price.
inexhaustible	ĭn ĕx ḥạust′ ĭ blе	never-ending; incapable of being exhausted.
inimitable	ĭn ĭm′ ĭt à blе	not able to be copied.
movable	mọv′ à blе	not fixed or stationary.
permissible	pĕr mĭs′ sĭ blе	allowable; not forbidden.
pleasurable	pleas′ ur à blе (plĕzh ēr)	capable of giving pleasure.
portable	pōrt′ à blе	convenient to transport.
preferable	prĕf′ ēr à blе	more to be desired.
reputable	rĕp′ ū tà blе	of good repute or character.
respectable	rĕ spĕet′ à blе	worthy of regard or honor.
reversible	rĕ vērs′ ĭ blе	able to be turned backward.
suitable	sūit′ à blе	appropriate; fitting; proper.
tangible	tăn′ ġĭ blе	real; solid and substantial.
terrible	tĕr′ rĭ blе	arousing awe or dread.
tractable	trăe′ tà blе	pliant; governable; docile.

Refer to a dictionary for definition, pronunciation, and use of:

alterable, impassable, impassible, incapable, insensible.

The suffixes *able and ible* are used to indicate "able to, fit to be, worthy to be, inclined to, or capable of being;" as, *readable*, capable of being read; *soluble*, capable of being solved; *lovable*, worthy of being loved; *perishable*, liable to perish. Both suffixes have the same meaning.

There is no royal rule for determining when to use *able* and when to use *ible*. However, words ending in *able* are much more common than those ending in *ible*.

The Suffixes able and ible

abominable	à bŏm′ ĭ nà ble	hateful; detestable.
admirable	ăd′ mĭ rà ble	worthy to be admired.
combustible	eŏm bŭs′ tĭ ble	inflammable; easy to burn.
corruptible	eŏr rŭpt′ ĭ ble	weak enough to be corrupted.
defensible	dĕ fĕn′ sĭ ble	capable of being defended.
divisible	dĭ vĭṣ′ ĭ ble	capable of being separated.
durable	dū′ rà ble	lasting, not changeable.
equitable	ĕq′ uĭ tà ble	fair; just in all dealings.
favorable	fā′ vŏr à ble	advantageous; promising.
flexible	flĕx′ ĭ ble	easily bent without breaking.
forcible	fōr′ çĭ ble	with force; powerful; strong.
impossible	ĭm pŏs′ sĭ ble	not capable of being done.
incredible	ĭn ered′ ĭ ble	unbelievable.
inevitable	ĭn ĕv′ ĭ tà ble	unavoidable.
irritable	ĭr′ rĭ tà ble	easily made angry; irascible.
justifiable	jŭs′ tĭ fī à ble	capable of being justified.
laughable	laugh′ à ble (läf)	funny; mirth-provoking.
perceptible	pĕr çĕp′ tĭ ble	discernible.
perishable	pĕr′ ĭsh à ble	liable to decay or to spoil.
plausible	plạu′ ṣĭ ble	worthy of belief or approval.
pliable	plī′ à ble	flexible; easily bent.
regrettable	rĕ grĕt′ tà ble	to be remembered with distress.
responsible	rĕ spŏn′ sĭ ble	reliable; trustworthy.
taxable	tăx′ à ble	subject to or may be taxed.
valuable	văl′ ũ à ble	of considerable worth or price.

Refer to a dictionary for definition, pronunciation, and use of:

creditable, dishonorable, habitable, redeemable, unavoidable.

Equity is a branch of the law that provides a remedy when not otherwise provided under the common law.   There were certain defects in the common law and to correct these inequalities a supplementary system of law known as equity developed in England.

Equitable right is a natural right or justice and this right can be enforced in a court of equity.

Synonyms for equity are: right, honest, upright, impartial, just, reasonable, justice.

The Suffixes able and ible

adorable	à dōr′ à ble	worthy of worship or love.
advisable	ăd vīz̧′ à ble	right and proper to be done.
applicable	ăp′ plĭ eà ble	able to be applied; suitable.
audible	au′ dĭ ble	loud enough to be heard.
blamable	blām′ à ble	deserving of censure; faulty.
capable	eā′ pà ble	having general ability to do.
censurable	çĕn′ sur à ble (shĕr)	deserving reproach or blame.
comparable	eŏm′ pà rà ble	worthy of being compared.
contemptible	eŏn tĕmpt′ ĭ ble	despicable; worthless; beggardly.
culpable	eŭl′ pà ble	deserving of censure or blame.
curable	eūr′ à ble	relating to healing.
destructible	dĕ strŭet′ ĭ ble	capable of being destroyed.
excusable	ĕx eūz̧′ à ble	that which may be forgiven.
feasible	fēa′ z̧ĭ ble	possible.
incompatible	ĭn eŏm păt′ ĭ ble	not able to act together.
infallible	ĭn făl′ lĭ ble	incapable of erring.
inflexible	ĭn flĕx′ ĭ ble	unyielding; firm.
invincible	ĭn vĭn′ çĭ ble	unconquerable.
invisible	ĭn vĭz̧′ ĭ ble	undiscernible.
irresistible	ĭr′ rĕ z̧ĭst ĭ ble	resistless.
liable	lī′ à ble	accountable or responsible.
negligible	nĕg′ lĭ ġĭ ble	not worthy of attention.
notable	nō′ tà ble	worthy of note; remarkable.
pitiable	pĭt′ ĭ à ble	arousing sympathy; pitiful.
traceable	trāçe′ à ble	capable of being followed.

Refer to a dictionary for definition, pronunciation, and use of:

incorrigible, laudable, reliable, susceptible, tolerable.

The suffix *able* is the form added to words of Anglo-Saxon origin. The suffix *ible* occurs mostly with words derived from the Latin. There are many exceptions to this rule, however, and the only sure way to know which form to use is to be able to spell the words correctly.

Able and *ible* are adjective suffixes.

Tendency to Add Extra Letters

altogether	ạl tọ gĕt̶h̶′ ẽr	entirely; without exception.
almost	ạl′ mōst	nearly; very nearly; all but.
anoint	à noint′	consecrate by applying oil.
barrel	băr′ rĕl	round, bulging wooden vessel.
benefited	bĕn′ ĕ fĭt ĕd	giving or receiving help.
denounce	dĕ nounç*e*′	speak against; openly accuse.
diligence	dĭl′ ĭ ġĕnç*e*	perseverance.
drowned	drown*e*d	died from suffocation.
hunger	hŭŋ′ gẽr	strong desire or craving.
later	lāt′ ẽr	after a lapse of time.
latter	lăt′ tẽr	more recent in time.
linen	lĭn′ ĕn	fine fabric made from flax.
linger	lĭŋ′ gẽr	delay; loiter.
mistaken	mĭs tāk′ *e*n	incorrect; wrong in judgment.
mistress	mĭs′ trĕss	woman head of a household.
obliging	ð̵ blīg̵′ ĭng	willing to do a kindness.
pigeon	pĭ′ ġeȯn	dove, wild or domesticated.
presently	prĕ꜡′ ĕnt lῠ	at once or without delay.
shining	shĭn′ ĭng	giving forth light; radiant.
sizable	sīz′ à bl*e*	of suitable bulk; fairly large.
umbrella	ŭm brĕl′ là	screen from rain, sun, etc.
using	ū꜡′ ĭng	employing for a purpose.
welcome	wĕl′ ȯ̵om*e*	received with gladness.
welfare	wĕl′ fâr*e*	well-being; prosperity.
wisdom	wĭ꜡′ dȯm	power of judging rightly.

Refer to a dictionary for definition, pronunciation, and use of:

breath,   breathe,   disastrous,   rostrum,   usual.

Assets (plural), all that one owns. It is derived from a French word, *assez*, meaning "enough." Originally it was a term applied to the estate of a deceased person, which in the hands of his heirs or executors, was sufficient (or enough) to pay the debts and legacies. Hence, it was the property of a deceased person subject by law to pay his debts and legacies. Now the term includes all the property of a person, a firm, or an estate available for the payment of debts. When used in a singular form it refers to any item of one's property.

Tendency to Omit Letters

accustom	ăe eŭs′ tòm	make familiar by much use.
aggregate	ăg′ grĕ găte	total sum taken together.
agreeable	à grēē′ à ble	pleasant; entirely willing.
channel	chăn′ nĕl	bed or course of a stream.
collection	eŏl lĕe′ tion	group assembled together.
compelled	eŏm pĕlled′	coerced; forced to yield.
co-operation	eŏ-ŏp′ ĕr ā tion	working jointly together.
depressed	dĕ pressed′ (prĕst)	dejected; dispirited.
forgiveness	fŏr gĭve′ nĕss	readiness to pardon.
generally	ġĕn′ ĕr ăl lў	for the most part; usually.
immediate	ĭm mē′ dĭ ate (ĭt)	without delay; direct; next.
noticeable	nō′ tĭçe à ble	capable of being observed.
occupation	ŏe eŭ pā′ tion	regular business or calling.
opposite	ŏp′ pŏ şĭte	diametrically different.
pressure	pres′ sure (prĕsh′ ĕr)	exertion of continuous force.
promissory	prŏm′ ĭs sō rў	containing an agreement.
quarreling	quạr′ rĕl ĭng	carrying on a wordy dispute.
really	rē′ ăl lў	as a matter of fact; actually.
reconciliation	rĕe ŏn çĭl ĭ ā′ tion	restoration to harmony.
recurrence	rĕ eûr′ rĕnçe	act of returning; return.
refinement	rĕ fīne′ mĕnt	polished manners; culture.
stubborn	stŭb′ bōrn	headstrong or obstinate.
sufficient	sŭf fĭ′ ciĕnt (shĕnt)	enough for one's needs.
suppose	sŭp pōşe′	assume as true; conjecture.
temptation	tĕmp tā′ tion	that which leads one astray.

Refer to a dictionary for definition, pronunciation, and use of:

employ, employe, employee, forgetting, stretching.

Coined words are words that have been made up to meet a real or a fancied need. Some coined words are used in business for advertising purposes, others in humorous writing or speaking. Some are made from foreign words and others are compounded from English words. Eventually many of them through long usage are graduated into good usage. Some common coinages are: *Chevrolet, nonskid, sundae, Fordism, corona, Hotpoint, Mazda,* and many others. Compile a list from the advertising section of a magazine.

Tendency to Omit Letters

addition	ăd dĭ′ tion	increase of any kind.
afford	ăf fōrd′	to be able to pay for or buy.
apprehend	ăp prĕ hĕnd′	arrest; understand; fear.
arrangement	ăr rān*ge*′ mĕnt	way in which things are placed.
bulletin	bu̯l′ lĕ tĭn	brief official report.
connection	e̯ŏn nĕe′ tion	state of being associated.
decent	dē′ çĕnt	acting in a proper way; modest.
descend	dĕ scĕnd′	go or come down; move down.
descent	dĕ scĕnt′	downward path; downward slope.
difficult	dĭf′ fĭ e̯ŭlt	hard to be done or manage.
diffident	dĭf′ fĭ dĕnt	modest; bashful; reserved.
embalm	ĕm bä*l*m′	preserve from decay.
innumerable	ĭn nū′ mĕr ȧ ble	too many to be counted.
jealous	jĕ*al*′ ou̯s	feeling envy or suspicion.
kingdom	kĭng′ dȯm	country ruled by a king.
marriageable	măr′ rĭa*ge* ȧ ble	suitable for wedlock.
opportunity	ŏp pŏr tū′ nĭ tў	fit place or favorable time.
pleasant	plĕa*ş*′ ănt	pleasing; agreeable; cheerful.
safety	sāfe′ tў	freedom from risk or danger.
sample	săm′ ple	part representing the whole.
slippery	slĭp′ pĕr ў	smooth; hard to stand on.
success	su̯e çĕss′	prosperity; good fortune.
tattler	tăt′ tlĕr	teller of tales or secrets.
tremendous	trĕ mĕn′ dou̯s	very great, large, or powerful.
useful	ūse′ fu̯l	full of practical worth.

Refer to a dictionary for definition, pronunciation, and use of:

native,   resign,   though,   thought,   through.

The verb *set* has more meanings than any other verb in the English language, according to Webster's Dictionary, where 105 meanings are listed.

According to the same authority, *run* is one of the most useful words, doing service as a noun, a verb, and an adjective, with ninety-five meanings.

Draw and *break* rank high with sixty-four definitions each.

Common Words Frequently Misspelled

advice	ăd vīçe′	instruction; counsel; caution.
arouse	à rouṣe′	stir up; excite to action.
arrival	ăr rī′ văl	coming to a place.
attract	ăt trăet′	allure; entice; draw to.
barbarous	bär′ bà roŭs	uncivilized; like a savage.
barrier	băr′ rĭ ēr	obstacle obstructing progress.
because	bĕ ɛauṣe′	since, for the reason that.
behavior	bĕ hāv′ ior (yēr)	manner of demeanor; conduct.
bountiful	boun′ tĭ fu̇l	liberal in giving.
camera	ɛăm′ ēr à	device for taking pictures.
career	ɛà rēer′	course of progress in life.
caress	ɛà rĕss′	act showing fondness or love.
catarrh	ɛà tärr*h*′	inflamed condition of the nose.
circumference	çĭr ɛŭm′ fēr ĕnçe	boundary line of a circle.
compliance	ɛŏm plī′ ănçe	act of consenting.
conceal	ɛŏn çēal′	hide or keep out of sight.
concentrate	ɛŏn′ çĕn trāte	press into a smaller space.
conference	ɛon′ fēr ĕnçe	meeting for a consultation.
continually	ɛŏn tĭn′ ṳ ăl lў	without intermission.
courageous	ɛoŭ rā′ ǵeoŭs	brave or full of daring.
ideal	ī dē′ ăl	existing in the mind only.
identity	ī dĕn′ tĭ tў	personal or individual self.
implement	ĭm′ plĕ mĕnt	tool, instrument, or utensil.
inexperience	ĭn ĕx pē′ rĭ ĕnçe	want of knowledge or skill.
satisfactory	săt′ ĭs făɛ tŏ rў	leaving no room for complaint.

Refer to a dictionary for definition, pronunciation, and use of:

courtesy,   cruelty,   cupidity,   substantial,   technical.

Furniture refers to and includes movable articles, such as beds, chairs, tables, cabinets, desks, and stoves. It is frequently classified as kitchen furniture, living-room furniture, office furniture. There is a distinction between *furniture* and *furnishings.*

Originally not only the movable articles and ornaments were called furniture, but also the personal outfit of clothing, jewelry, arms, and the like. It still retains some of the early significance in the advertisement of "men's furnishings."

Common Words Frequently Misspelled

apathy	ăp′ à thў	absence or want of feeling.
appeal	ăp pēal′	earnest or urgent request.
appearance	ăp pēar′ ănçe	act of becoming visible.
applied	ăp plīed′	employed or put to use.
approval	ăp prọv′ ăl	ratification; commendation.
community	eŏm mū′ nĭ tў	public; society in general.
credited	erĕd′ ĭt ĕd	placed to the account of.
elegant	ĕl′ ĕ gănt	graceful; refined; tasteful.
excessive	ĕx çĕs′ sĭve	much too high; immoderate.
fuel	fū′ ĕl	heat-producing substance.
fundamental	fŭn dà mĕn′ tăl	serving as a base; essential.
futile	fū′ tĭle	useless; vain; ineffectual.
genius	ġēn′ ius (yŭs)	one having superior talents.
gesture	ġĕs′ tụre	expressive body motion.
haughty	hạugh′ tў	proud; disdainful; overbearing.
identical	ī dĕn′ tĭ eăl	exactly alike or equal.
impartial	ĭm pär′ tial (shăl)	fair; treating everyone alike.
intolerable	ĭn tŏl′ ẽr à ble	not capable of being endured.
isolated	ī′ sỏ lāt ĕd	placed apart from others.
journal	joûr′ năl	daily record; daybook.
legitimate	lĕ ġĭt′ ĭ mate (ĭt)	according to law; genuine.
lovable	lŏv′ à ble	amiable; worthy of love.
opinion	ỏ pĭn′ ion (yŭn)	what one believes; notion.
optometrist	ŏp tŏm′ ĕ trĭst	one who fits glasses.
pursuit	pūr sūit′	chasing after; occupation.

Refer to a dictionary for definition, pronunciation, and use of:

furnish,   mosquito,   mustache,   muzzle,   oblige.

A *slogan* is a catch phrase or motto adopted by a manufacturer, business house, political party, or other enterprise for advertising purposes. It is derived from the Gaelic "Slaughghairm" a clan-rallying cry for summoning men to battle. The right to make or use a slogan is generally regarded as belonging to the one who first adopted it.

An *antonym* is a word having an opposite meaning to another word; as agile, clumsy; believe, deny; well, ill; kind, cruel; legal, illegal.

Common Words Frequently Misspelled

actually	ăc t̤ŭ ăl lў	as a matter of fact.
assure	ăs sṳre′	make sure or certain.
decency	dē′ çĕn çў	fitness; appropriateness.
deferred	dĕ fērred′	"put off until another day."
ignorant	ĭg′ nŏ rănt	lacking knowledge; untaught.
impropriety	ĭm prŏ prī′ ĕ tў	fact of being improper.
infancy	ĭn′ făn çў	early childhood; babyhood.
instinctive	ĭn stĭnc′ tĭve	natural or innate impulse.
loveliness	lŏve′ lĭ nĕss	beautifulness.
penetrate	pĕn′ ĕ trāte	gain entrance into; pierce.
perseverance	pēr sĕ vēr′ ănçe	steadfastness in purpose.
ponderous	pŏn′ dĕr oŭs	of great weight; heavy.
pretext	prē′ tĕxt	excuse; fictitious reason.
prevail	prĕ vāil′	secure an advantage; overcome.
proclamation	prŏe là mā′ tion	official announcement.
rigorous	rĭg′ ŏr oŭs	severe; strict; inclement.
scrupulous	serṳ′ pŭ loŭs	conscientious in small matters.
slaughter	sl̤augh′ tēr	violent destruction of life.
stationary	stā′ tion ar ў (ĕr)	fixed in a certain place.
superficial	sū pēr fĭ′ cial (shăl)	on the surface; shallow.
suspense	sŭs pĕnse′	state of uncertainty.
temperament	tĕm′ pēr à mĕnt	mental and physical make-up.
temperance	tĕm′ pēr ănçe	moderation; self-restraint.
universal	ū nĭ vēr′ săl	belonging to all mankind.
wonder	wŏn′ dēr	something extraordinary.

Refer to a dictionary for definition, pronunciation, and use of:

accordance,   pleasant,   pretentious,   propagate,   wrestle.

Infants. From a legal viewpoint, infants are persons under the age of twenty-one years. They are commonly referred to as "minors." In some states, by statutory law, women are deemed of age at eighteen, and in some jurisdictions (for some purposes) minors are considered of age upon marriage. The law makes no distinction between infants of tender or mature age so far as their legal capacity to make enforceable contracts is concerned.

Common Words Frequently Misspelled

absent	ăb′ sĕnt	not present; away; missing.
adversity	ăd vẽr′ sĭ tỹ	ill fortune; affliction.
asylum	à sȳ′ lŭm	place of refuge; a retreat.
buried	bur′ ĭed (bĕr)	placed in a grave; covered.
clumsy	elŭm′ şỹ	lacking in skill or grace.
controversy	eŏn′ trŏ vẽr sỹ	dispute; contention; quarrel.
cushion	eụsh′ ion (ŭn)	soft, stuffed pillow or pad.
cylinder	çỹl′ ĭn dẽr	circular hollow vessel.
dependent	dĕ pĕnd′ ĕnt	relying on someone else.
describe	dĕ serībe′	explain; give an account of.
disagreeable	dĭs à grēē′ à ble	unsatisfactory or offensive.
discharge	dĭs chärġe′	dismissal from employment.
elementary	ĕl ĕ mĕn′ tà rỹ	relating to first principles.
enormous	ĕ nôr′ moŭs	excessive in size or degree.
entitled	ĕn tī′ tled	having a claim or right.
indelible	ĭn dĕl′ ĭ ble	that which cannot be erased.
inferior	ĭn fē′ rĭ õr	lower in place or rank.
launch	launch (lônch)	open, power-driven boat.
metallic	mĕ tăl′ lĭe	of or pertaining to a metal.
popular	pŏp′ ụ lär	"pleasing to the people."
possible	pŏs′ sĭ ble	liable to happen; feasible.
simplicity	sĭm plĭç′ ĭ tỹ	plainness; clearness; honesty.
tragedy	trăġ′ ĕ dỹ	dire or dreadful happening.
visible	vĭş′ ĭ ble	capable of being seen.
wooden	wŏŏd′ ĕn	consisting of wood; clumsy.

Refer to a dictionary for definition, pronunciation, and use of:

dependent, disposition, distinguish, exterior, extinct.

A *"kangaroo court"* is a slang expression for an unauthorized and irresponsible tribunal acting without authority, and in disregard of principles of law and justice. In other words, it is a sham court or a mock trial. It is particularly applied to a trial conducted by prisoners for punishing minor offenses among themselves or for the purpose of obtaining illicit fines. Lately the term has come to be applied to petty local courts presided over by duly elected officials who receive fees only in case the defendant is convicted. The defendant is usually convicted.

Monosyllables Commonly Misspelled

LESSON 123

coarse, thick; rude; rough.
course, path or track.
dome, vaulted roof.
dunce, dull-witted person.
flea, small wingless insect.
flee, fly away.
freak, monstrosity.
laud, praise highly.
lose, mislay; overlook.
myth, legend; fable.
nose, organ of smell.
nurse, nourish; nurture.
pulp, soft part of fruit.
quail, shrink from; cower.
queer, odd or peculiar.
scour, cleanse by friction.
seam, joining line.
seem, appear.
sharp, having a keen edge.
since, after; because.
soak, wet thoroughly.
touch, come in contact with.
waist, part of the body.
waste, refuse; useless.
yeast, fermentation fungus.

LESSON 124

arch, bowlike curve.
bail, surety or security.
bale, bundle.
boil, bubble up with heat.
broil, cook over coals.
charge, debit; accuse.
crave, desire greatly.
dawn, "break o'day."
faint, weak; languid.
feint, deceptive motion.
fetch, go after and bring.
flock, collection of animals.
herb, plant with soft stem.
lung, organ of respiration.
nail, metal fastening pin.
oath, solemn affirmation.
parch, scorch or burn.
plight, embarrassment.
price, what has to be paid.
scorch, burn; parch; sear.
soil, earth; make dirty.
throat, part of the neck.
which, interrogative pronoun.
whirl, rapid revolving motion.
witch, evil spirit; a hag.

Refer to a dictionary for definition, pronunciation, and use of:

fete, pert, quake, scarce, vain, vane, vein, whim.

Silent letters are valuable in determining the meaning of many words having similar sounds as *scent* and *sent*; *whole* and *hole*; *two*, *too*, and to; *jam* and *jamb*. Are there others?

A prize was once offered any member of an educational institution who would write and spell correctly the words in the following sentence:

"It is an agreeable sight to witness the unparalleled embarrassment of a harassed peddler attempting to gauge the symmetry of a peeled onion, which a sibyl had stabbed with a poniard, regardless of its cornelian hue."

118

Monosyllables Commonly Misspelled

LESSON 125

burst, break by violence.
cleat, strip of wood or iron.
coast, seashore.
cough, expulsion of breath.
crowd, mass of people.
daub, smear; plaster.
disk, flat circular plate.
feud, bitter strife.
forth, forward or onward.
found, discovered.
hinge, door hanger.
knack, readiness; aptness.
moan, low groan.
mine, belonging to me.
plate, flat, shallow dish.
prone, with face downward.
rinse, cleanse in water.
scheme, plan; method.
search, seek; look for.
solve, obtain a result.
spade, implement for digging.
stain, discoloration.
trout, game fish.
urge, impel; stimulate.
wrath, violent anger.

LESSON 126

bare, without covering.
bear, wild animal.
bask, lie in warmth.
basque, short-skirted bodice.
crown, top of anything.
death, end of life.
feast, elaborate meal.
fleece, sheep's coat of wool.
fleet, swift or nimble.
flint, hard stone.
foam, froth; scum.
forge, imitate falsely.
funds, available assets.
gust, sudden squall of wind.
made, produced.
maid, unmarried girl.
moist, damp; slightly wet.
peck, eight quarts.
plain, simple, not elaborate.
plane, level surface.
pitch, resinous substance.
sauce, dressing or relish.
school, place of instruction.
small, having little size.
sneer, show contempt.

Refer to a dictionary for definition, pronunciation, and use of:

pole, poll;   shear, sheer;   steal, steel;   through, threw.

The *copperhead* is a poisonous snake somewhat allied to the rattlesnake, but without rattles. It strikes without giving warning. It is found in many parts of the eastern United States. The term "copperhead" was applied to persons in the Northern States who were secretly in sympathy with the Confederates and rendered them aid to the detriment of the Union cause.

Monosyllables Commonly Misspelled

LESSON 127

alms, relief to the poor.
bathe, wash by immersion.
blush, reddening of the skin.
brawn, muscular strength.
chair, movable seat.
churn, stir violently.
cloak, outer garment.
coat, man's garment.
crime, violation of law.
debt, what one owes.
film, thin covering or layer.
fraud, deception or deceit.
jest, joke; wit.
lace, network made of thread.
leak, trickle through.
luck, good or bad fortune.
noun, word used as a name.
proud, haughty or arrogant.
puff, short, quick blast.
quick, swift; prompt; alert.
scrub, cleanse by rubbing.
shave, cut with an edged tool.
smirch, smear; make dirty.
smirk, smile conceitedly.
wry, distorted; twisted.

LESSON 128

bark, covering of a tree.
baste, sew loosely.
blond, fair complexion.
brave, courageous; daring.
chew, grind with the teeth.
coal, substance used for fuel.
crease, mark of a fold.
farce, exaggerated comedy.
frame, skeleton of a structure.
gaunt, lank; haggard; thin.
geese, plural of goose.
hump, rounded knob.
learn, acquire knowledge.
mode, method; way; style.
null, of no effect or force.
pawn, pledge.
pearl, lustrous jewel.
rave, talk wildly.
scar, mark or blemish.
scum, refuse; anything vile.
slope, incline; slant.
surge, swell of the sea.
tease, torment or tantalize.
tongue, organ of taste.
turf, upper stratum of earth.

Refer to a dictionary for definition, pronunciation, and use of:

chant;   pale, pail;   realm;   strait, straight;   vice, vise.

Overworked or shopworn words. Many useful words have been used so often that they have become threadbare, and have little meaning anymore. A current list of such words include: *cute, clever, fierce, grand, gorgeous, lurid, meticulous, succeed, fast, horrid, splendid, sure, very, wonderful, reaction, motivate, hectic, swell, dandy,* and the like. These words all have a definite meaning, and should not be used indiscriminately. Such use is an indication of a poverty of vocabulary.

Monosyllables Commonly Misspelled

LESSON 129

boil, heat highly.
brought, did bring.
calm, still; quiet; peaceful.
cede, give up; yield.
crisp, brittle; firm and fresh.
crude, raw; unrefined.
dance, move rhythmically.
droop, hang downward.
fear, feeling of danger.
fork, pronged utensil.
fret, vexation; worry.
fringe, ornamental border.
hearse, funeral vehicle.
heart, organ of the body.
neck, narrow part.
noise, sound of any kind.
pace, step or stride.
scold, chide; find fault.
shirk, avoid an obligation.
shun, avoid; keep clear of.
size, dimension or magnitude.
skill, expertness; dexterity.
speak, talk; converse.
stage, elevated platform.
vamp, upper front of shoe.

LESSON 130

brawl, noisy fight.
break, separate into parts.
brogue, dialect; accent.
catch, overtake; grasp.
chafe, fret; vex; excite.
cinch, strong saddle girth.
cleanse, free from filth.
cringe, wince; shrink.
curb, restrain.
flask, small, flat bottle.
foil, defeat; outwit.
gauze, thin, light fabric.
glimpse, hurried view.
greedy, ravenous; very eager.
quote, name as authority.
roast, cook by exposure to fire.
scratch, wound lightly.
sear, burn; dry up; wither.
sense, good judgment.
source, origin; first cause.
spasm, sudden paroxysm.
speed, rapidity; dispatch.
squall, sudden burst of wind.
trough, long tray.
vault, storage space.

Refer to a dictionary for definition, pronunciation, and use of:

blue, blew;   e'er, air, heir;   wave, waive;   whole, hole.

Growing crops. Annual crops are the product of the earth, produced annually by planting and cultivation. In law they are known as "emblements" and include corn, wheat, oats, garden vegetables, and the like. They are deemed personal property. The fruit of trees, and perennial plants, however, are considered a part of the real property until they are severed.

Do not add a *t* to *specimen*, in analogy with words ending in *ment*.

121

Monosyllables Commonly Misspelled

LESSON 131

acre, 160 square rods.
bawl, cry loudly.
blast, blow to pieces.
chain, links joined together.
choice, preference; select.
cream, fat of milk.
dusk, twilight.
earn, acquire by effort.
fact, anything true.
fame, renown; reputation.
frail, fragile; easily broken.
grease, soft, animal fat.
guile, deceit; cunning; fraud.
heave, lift or raise upward.
husk, outer covering.
know, perceive or understand.
league, confederation.
mean, average; contemptible.
mince, chop very fine.
numb, without feeling.
pick, choose; select.
rough, crude, not smooth.
scale, utensil for weighing.
thrill, feel a sharp sensation.
wreath, twisted band of
  flowers.

LESSON 132

browse, feed on grass.
bruise, injure; crush.
chaff, husks of grain.
claw, scratch; scrape.
dearth, scarcity; deficiency.
edge, side; border; margin.
gown, loose, outer garment.
grace, charm; beauty.
guide, show the way.
haste, speed; hurry; rapidity.
hatch, produce from eggs.
leaf, thin sheet of paper.
loan, permission to use.
lynch, hang unlawfully a suspected person.
meat, food in general.
much, great in quantity.
pack, stow away.
phrase, group of words.
plume, ornamental feather.
prim, neat; nice in dress.
prime, first in rank.
prince, man of high rank.
rain, condensed vapor.
reign, rule, as of a sovereign.
sphere, globe; round body.

Refer to a dictionary for definition, pronunciation, and use of:

chose, choose, curt, flout, pith, raze, raise, rove, sleek.

A *doublet* in English refers to pairs of words which have arisen from the same original form but have diverged in both form and sense. Some of the most common doublets are: *yard* and *garden; worm* and *vermin; rear* and *raise; girdle* and *girth; will* and *testament; give* and *devise; naked* and *nude; abbreviate* and *abridge; compute* and *count; secure* and *sure; fragile* and *frail;* and many others. Many of these doublets are due to borrowing from other languages.

Monosyllables Commonly Misspelled

LESSON 133

brusque, abrupt in manner.
burnt, consumed by fire.
chide, reprove; censure; scold.
cost, price paid.
duct, tube, pipe or canal.
flog, punish with blows.
game, sport; wild animals.
hence, from now or here.
joke, jest; funny saying.
juice, sap; fluid part.
leave, go away from.
limp, walk lamely.
mock, imitate; deride.
pique, slight anger.
purge, make clean or pure.
scourge, whip or lash.
shout, loud outcry.
slave, one who is in bondage.
snub, intentional slight.
spread, cover or overlay.
tired, weary; exhausted.
verb, part of speech.
verge, extreme edge.
wealth, riches; abundance.
whet, make sharp or keen.

LESSON 134

bulge, bend outward.
cant, jargon; slang.
chute, inclined trough.
coin, minted metal money.
drain, draw off by degrees.
drill, bore; pierce; perforate.
erg, unit of energy.
fault, error; wrong action.
glance, quick look.
globe, ball; sphere; the earth.
hoard, amass a treasure.
jerk, sharp, quick pull.
peeve, annoy or vex.
probe, investigate; examine.
roar, loud, continuous noise.
rogue, dishonest person.
rouge, cosmetic material.
saint, holy person.
seethe, boil; bubble over.
shame, disgrace, dishonor.
shrewd, clever; keen-sighted.
skip, light leap or bound.
slough, place of deep mire.
stalk, stem of a plant.
wince, flinch; shrink back.

Refer to a dictionary for definition, pronunciation, and use of:

croup, crop; feat, feet; rice, rise; shone, shown.

Viz. is the abbreviation of a Latin word, *videlicit,* meaning "namely," "it is easy to see," or "one may see." It is now translated as "to wit" or "namely" and is so used. Ordinarily the abbreviation has no pronunciation so that the word in full is read.

Character is what a person is; *reputation* is what his neighbors think he is. The first word refers to the person himself while the second word refers to what is in the minds of others.

Monosyllables Commonly Misspelled

LESSON 135

ache, sensation of pain.
brand, mark; a burning stick.
bribe, corrupt by a gift.
bulk, magnitude or size.
coke, coal deprived of gas.
faith, firm belief or trust.
feet, plural of foot.
fleet, swift in motion.
frost, frozen dew.
gist, material part.
haze, light mist or smoke.
pain, ache; bodily suffering.
purse, small moneybag.
quilt, bed coverlet.
quite, entirely or completely.
quiz, question closely.
range, extent; reach; scope.
sack, bag; plunder; pillage.
smoke, gaseous sooty vapor.
spurn, treat with contempt.
stile, series of steps.
style, mode; fashion; conduct.
taunt, jibe or jeer.
thirst, craving or longing.
tract, large or small area.

LESSON 136

bland, soft; mild; gentle.
clamp, hold firmly together.
dose, quantity of medicine.
doze, sleep lightly.
fence, inclosing structure.
float, keep from sinking.
gate, opening in a fence.
ghoul, grave robber.
gilt, yellow like gold.
guilt, crime; sin; wickedness.
hail, frozen rain.
hoax, trick; practical joke.
main, principal; chief.
maul, heavy hammer.
mold, shape or fashion.
mould, same as mold.
quaint, odd; old-fashioned.
rout, defeat disastrously.
snarl, surly expression.
terse, concise; pithy.
twirl, turn around quickly.
vague, indefinite; uncertain.
whack, resounding blow.
youth, young lad.
zinc, bluish white metal.

Refer to a dictionary for definition, pronunciation, and use of:

brood, brewed; bride; blink; pall; peal, peel; taut, taught.

A *proxy* may be a person or it may be an authoritative document. Under the common law a stockholder in a corporation was not permitted to vote in corporate matters unless present in person. Under the modern law a member of a corporation may authorize another to officiate for him in his absence by voting the shares of the absent member. This right is called "voting by proxy."

Changed Meanings

abrupt (break off),[1] sudden; hasty; unceremonious.

accost (rib to rib), speak to first; address or greet.

affront (strike on the forehead), insult; hurt one's feelings.

allege (bring forward as evidence), bring forward as a reason.

alone (all+one), without anyone or anything else; oneself.

ambition (canvassing for votes), strong desire for power or fame.

amuse (waste time), entertain in a pleasing manner; entertain.

ancestor (one who goes before), one from whom a person is descended.

anecdote (not published), short entertaining story or incident.

appeal (make pale), call for a decision; request earnestly.

artifice (handicraft), an artful or skillful trick; trickery; plot.

bargain (carry goods in a boat), mutual agreement between parties.

bashful (expressing astonishment), very modest.

belfry (watchtower), room in which a bell is or may be hung.

bombast (cotton padding), high-sounding language; claptrap.

breakfast (break+fast), early morning meal; first meal.

broker (retailer of wine), one employed to buy or sell for others.

burglar (town-thief), one who breaks into a house to rob.

carbuncle (burning coal), inflamed local ulcer or tumor.

carnival (meatless time), generally a festival; season of merriment.

carpenter (carriage-maker), builder of houses; worker in wood.

cartoon (pasteboard), humorous illustration; pictorial caricature.

champion (fighter), successful contestant; winner of a prize.

chapel (short cloak or hood), church or room for worship.

clerk (clergyman), one employed to keep records; salesman.

There are words that have an opposite meaning in many cases. Note that the word *dispatch* may refer to a message sent with speed, or it may pertain to putting a person to death.

It is well-known that "to dress a person" is to put on more clothes while "to dress poultry" is to remove their covering.

A *blackberry* may be in some instances either white or red.

Meat may be the flesh of animals or it may be anything eaten as food. What is the meaning of *sweetmeat?* Does it have different meanings? Check it with *sweetbread.*

---

[1]The original or literal meaning is enclosed in parentheses.

Changed Meanings

censure (value; tax),[1] expression of fault-finding; blame.

companion (storeroom for bread), one who associates with another.

compile (plunder), collect material to form a book.

comrade (room or chamber), one who shares his fortunes with another.

congregation (political convention), assembly of persons.

constable (count of the stable), petty peace officer.

convert (turn), change from one thing or religion to another.

curriculum (race course), specified course of study in a school.

dangerous (power of a lord), unsafe; liability to harm.

deliberate (weight or balance), reflect upon; consider carefully.

destitute (foresaken), condition of want of necessaries.

discuss (shake apart), talk it over; reason upon.

dreary (bloody or gory), dismal; gloomy; cheerless.

eager (sharp; sour), strong desire to get or do; earnest.

error (wandering), blunder or mistake; an inaccuracy.

gazetteer (writer or journalist), geographical dictionary.

generous (of a noble race), liberal in giving; magnanimous.

gland (shaped like an acorn), secreting organ of the body.

gossip (sponsor in baptism), one who retails news or tells tales.

handsome (dexterous; handy), pleasing appearance; good looking.

hypocrite (actor), one who tries to appear what he is not.

idiot (private person), weak-minded person; ignorant person.

impertinent (not applicable), unbecoming in words or action.

insane (not healthy), mentally deranged; disordered in mind.

insolent (unusual behavior), very rude in speech; insulting.

The names of most of the living animals are derived from the English; as *ox, sheep, deer*. Words naming farm implements, such as the *spade, sickle*, and *flail*, and those words denoting relationship as *father, mother, son, daughter, husband*, and *wife* come to us through the English.

After the flesh of an animal is prepared for food, it is usually given a French name; as *beef, mutton, ven'son*, and *pork*. It is said the Englishman worked looking after the animals while they were alive, but the rich Normans ate the flesh when the animal was dead.

---

[1]The original or literal meaning is enclosed in parentheses.

Changed Meanings

instruct (build),[1] teach; give information or knowledge.
intoxicate (drug or poison), overstimulate with strong drink.
intuition (something seen by the soul), power of knowing; insight.
jockey (diminutive of Jock), one who rides horses in races.
jubilee (blast of a trumpet), state or season of general joy.
knave (boy or youth), cheat; person of low character.
leech (physician), blood-sucking worm.
legend (something to be read), story of bygone times.
manuscript (written by hand), now it may be typewritten.
martyr (witness), one who dies or suffers for his faith.
mathematics (disposed to learn), science of numbers and space.
mop (napkin), utensil for washing floors.
morsel (to bite), tasty dish; small meal; small quantity.
mortgage (dead pledge), conveyance of property as security.
muscle (little mouse), fleshy part of the body.
mystery (close the eyes), something wholly unknown.
naughty (worthless), wicked; mischievous; bad.
obvious (met in the way), easily seen or understood; evident.
officious (obliging), impertinent; meddlesome.
ordeal (judgment of God), severe test of character or endurance.
outrage (beyond), treat with great abuse.
painful (penalty), causing distress of mind or body.
parable (placing beside), narrative that teaches a moral lesson.
parade (preparation), formal march or procession.
paregoric (consoling with words), drug that soothes pain.

The word *fast* originally meant something firm or immovable. Now it may also mean the opposite: as moving rapidly. By referring to an unabridged dictionary we learn that a key is *fast* in a lock when we cannot get it out; a person runs *fast* when he moves rapidly. Colors are *fast* when they do not run, that is, when they are permanent and fixed. A person may eat *fast* or he may *fast* when he does not eat. An athletic field may be *fast* when it is said that the court is *fast*. One can live *fast*, and one's tears can fall *fast*. A minister can make a couple *fast* in wedlock.

[1]The original or literal meaning of each word in this lesson is inclosed in parentheses.

Changed Meanings

peevish (malignant),[1] showing ill nature or ill temper; fretful.
peremptory (destructive), allowing no question or delay.
perfunctory (discharge; get rid of), performed mechanically.
petticoat (small coat), loose underskirt worn by women.
precarious (obtained by prayer), depending upon another's will.
premature (before ripe), happening or developed too soon.
presume (take beforehand), take for granted; assume.
prevaricate (spread the legs apart in walking), tell an untruth.
prosecute (pursue), carry on a legal prosecution.
recipe (take back), directions for mixing or taking ingredients.
relevant (giving relief or help), applicable to the case in hand.
reprimand (press back), rebuke or reprove severely.
repudiate (be ashamed), have nothing to do with; cast off.
repugnant (fight against), strong dislike; distasteful; repulsive.
resign (break a seal), give up; withdraw from; quit.
retort (something bent back), quick, cutting, sharp reply.
rival (one who lives on the opposite side of a river), competitor.
sarcasm (bite the lips in rage), bitter, cutting remarks.
superstition (standover), belief in what is absurd without proof.
sympathy (suffering with another), fellow-feeling for another.
trivial (where three crossroads meet), unimportant.
urchin (hedgehog), playful term for a child; youngster.
vehement (out of one's mind), very earnest; eager or urgent.
vivacious (long-lived), animated; full of life; gay or lively.
wrangle (argue), noisy dispute or brawl; angry words.

Line fences have often been the cause of bitter quarrels and lawsuits between adjoining property owners. Likewise in primitive times there was no more fruitful source of contention than river-rights, not only for the use of the water but because the river furnished a natural boundary. Out of this situation we get the origin of the word *rival* (a competitor) as one who lived on the opposite side of a stream from another. The plural, *rivals*, was used to designate those who obtained water from the same brook. This often caused contention and the term came to be applied to the animosity that arose where different persons claimed superior water-rights.

---

[1]The original or literal meaning is enclosed in parentheses.

Words Derived from the Names of Persons or Places[1]

agate, precious stone; (the river "Achates" in Sicily).

artesian, flowing well from natural pressure; ("Artois," France).

assassin, murderer; ("Syrian" hashish, a drug causing insanity).

bantam, small domestic fowl; ("Bantam," in Java).

bedlam, scene of confusion; (St. Mary hospital in "Bethlehem").

cambric, fine, thin, white fabric; ("Cambray," a French city).

canter, moderate and easy gallop; (abbreviation of "Canterbury").

champagne, light sparkling wine; (providence of "Champagne," France).

cravat, necktie or neckcloth; (first worn by the "Croatians").

dollar, coin of the United States; (German thaler; valley).

epicure, one fond of good living; ("Epicurus," a Greek philosopher).

gauze, thin, transparent goods; ("Gaza," city in Palestine).

indigo, a deep, blue dye; ("Indicos," an Indian).

January, first month of the year; (Roman god, "Janus").

jovial, of a happy disposition; (born under the planet "Jupiter").

Madeira, wine; (made on the island of "Madeira").

mauve, delicate purple color; (from the French "Mallow," a paint).

meander, to wander aimlessly; ("Mainandros," a river in Asia).

milliner, maker of women's headdress; ("Milan," a city in Italy).

muslin, soft, cotton cloth; ("Mosul," city in Mesopotamia).

panic, sudden fear or fright; ("Pan," the god of the shepherds).

platonic, mental and spiritual love; ("Plato," a philosopher).

tantalize, to tease; ("Tantalus," condemned to the lower world).

tawdry, cheap and showy; ("St. Audrey," an English fair).

volcano, mountain belching fire; ("Vulcan," the god of fire).

Many words have an interesting historical background. The word *tantalize* given above is such a word. In Greek mythology Tantalus offended the gods. He was condemned to be placed in a lake whose waters reached to his chin, but receded when he sought to allay his thirst. The branches of the trees overhanging were laden with choice fruit; whenever he reached out his hand, the limbs of the trees, like the water, would recede out of his reach. What could be more tantalizing?

---

[1]The source of each word is indicated in the parentheses.

PART II

Miscellaneous Words

"Words are mighty; words are living."

—ADELAIDE PROCTOR.

LESSON 142

Miscellaneous Words

acquire	ăe quīre′	gain possession of; attain.
active	ăe′ tĭve	alert; busy.
all ready	ạll rĕad′ y̆	prepared for use.
all right	ạll rīght′	entirely correct.
already	ạl rĕad′ y̆	prior to some particular time.
arid	ăr′ ĭd	parched with heat; very dry.
auburn	au′ burn (bẽrn)	golden-brown color.
audacity	au dăç′ ĭ ty̆	bold; daring; impertinence.
available	à vāĭl′ à ble	ready; convenient; handy.
cemetery	çĕm′ ĕ tĕr y̆	place where dead are interred.
disappearance	dĭs ăp pēar′ ănçe	act of vanishing from sight.
discordant	dĭs eôrd′ ănt	harsh, not harmonious in sound.
endeavor	ĕn dĕav′ ŏr	attempt; make an effort to try.
executive	ĕx̱ ĕe′ û tĭve	having administrative ability.
ferocious	fĕ rō′ cious (shŭs)	extremely fierce; very savage.
impromptu	ĭm prŏmp′ tū	without previous preparation.
intercede	ĭn tẽr çēde′	plead for another; mediate.
landscape	lănd′ seāpe	picture of natural scenery.
loiter	loi′ tẽr	lag behind; hang about; linger.
necessity	nĕ cĕs′ sĭ ty̆	something very badly needed.
opaque	ŏ pāque′ (pāk′)	not able to be seen through.
palpable	păl′ pà ble	easily perceived and detected.
persuade	pẽr suade′ (swād′)	induce one to do something.
pretense	prĕ tĕnse′	pretext; false deception.
venturesome	vĕn′ ṱure sòme	daring; not afraid of danger.

Refer to a dictionary for definition, pronunciation, and use of:

physique,   proprietary,   trifle,   vulture,   whistle.

Silent letters serve many useful purposes. For instance, silent letters may be used to modify the sound of vowels and of consonants; as, *mad* and *made*, *plan* and *plane*, *sin* and *sign*, *rag* and *rage*, *ace* and *ache*. Endeavor to compile a list of other pairs of words showing how silent letters may be used to modify the meaning of words.

The spelling of the word *piece* will not be difficult if you will remember that the first three letters spell *pie*.

131

Miscellaneous Words

affectation	ăf fĕe tā′ tion	unnatural or artificial manner.
allusion	ăl lū′ sion (zhŭn)	casual indirect reference.
artificial	är tĭ fĭ′ cial (shăl)	unnatural; unreal.
color	eŏl′ ŏr	paint; appearance; tint.
conservation	eŏn sēr vā′ tion	act of preserving.
decision	dĕ çĭ′ sion (zhŭn)	definite conclusion.
descendant	dĕ scĕnd′ ănt	coming from another ancestor.
dilemma	dĭ lĕm′ mȧ	awkward or difficult choice.
diligent	dĭl′ ĭ ġĕnt	steady and earnest; painstaking.
elevator	ĕl′ ĕ vā tŏr	hoisting machine or cage.
entire	ĕn tīre′	complete in all its parts.
evident	ĕv′ ĭ dĕnt	clear or plain to the mind.
excel	ĕx çĕl′	surpass or outdo all others.
exemplify	ĕx̱ ĕm′ plĭ fȳ	illustrate by example.
fanatic	fȧ năt′ ĭe	wildly or unreasonably zealous.
formerly	fôr′ mēr lȳ	some time ago; heretofore.
fragment	frăg′ mĕnt	piece broken off; incomplete.
further	fûr′ thēr	beyond; more remote.
handle	hăn′ dle	part of a tool; touch or feel.
invention	ĭn vĕn′ tion	original plan or contrivance.
preference	prĕf′ ēr ĕnçe	choice of one over another.
routine	rọu tïne′	any regular course of duties.
spacious	spā′ cious (shŭs)	vast; very large in extent.
strenuous	strĕn′ û oŭs	energetic; vigorous; forceful.
subscription	sŭb serĭp′ tion	sum or amount of sums given or subscribed.

Refer to a dictionary for definition, pronunciation, and use of:

auspice, depleted, equipage, orphan, rancid.

Etymology is derived from a Greek word meaning "description." As commonly used it refers to the derivation, history, and meaning of words.

Silent letters are sometimes useful as an aid to indicate the origin or etymology of words; as *rhapsody, psychology, psychiatry, agnostic, mnemonics, phthisis, rhythm,* and the like.

Miscellaneous Words

ambitious	ăm bĭ′ tious (shŭs)	desirous of power or honor.
appease	ăp pēaṣe′	make quiet; pacify.
application	ăp plĭ ēā′ tion	attention to duty; diligence.
apprehension	ăp prĕ hĕn′ sion	anxiety; fear; dread.
benevolence	bĕ nĕv′ ô lĕnçe	quality of goodwill; kindness.
consequence	eŏn′ sĕ quĕnçe	that which naturally follows.
duplicity	dŭ plĭç′ ĭ tў	deceitfulness; falseness.
eradicate	ĕ răd′ ĭ eāte	wipe out or destroy entirely.
extract	ĕx trăet′	draw out; a tincture; essence.
extreme	ĕx trēme′	highest in degree; most urgent.
forbid	fôr bĭd′	prohibit; oppose; obstruct.
gracious	grā′ cious (shŭs)	polite; kind; affable.
heretofore	hēre tọ fōre′	up to this time; formerly.
herewith	hēre wĭth′	along with this.
hesitate	hĕṣ′ ĭ tāte	be in doubt about anything.
inability	ĭn à bĭl′ ĭ tў	want of power; incapacity.
inasmuch	ĭn ăṣ mŭch′	this being the case.
include	ĭn eludẹ′	contain as a part.
occurred	ŏe eûrred′	happened.
parallel	păr′ ăl lĕl	equally distant at all points.
portray	pōr trāy′	describe in words.
repel	rĕ pĕl′	drive or force back.
total	tō′ tăl	entire—not partial; undivided.
triumph	trī′ ŭmph	achievement; gain a victory.
uncertain	ŭn çêr′ taĭn	not sure or certain; doubtful.

Refer to a dictionary for definition, pronunciation, and use of:

commercial,   mentioned,   merely,   merit,   might.

The letter *b* is silent after *m* in the same syllable; as in *lamb, climb, comb, bomb, dumb, thumb*; but it is not silent in the word *rhomb*. It is also silent before *t*; as in *debt, doubt, subtle*, and others.

Do not pronounce the sound of *t* in *often*, nor in *listen*; the *l* in *calm*, nor in *folks;* the *w* in *wreck, wrack, wrong*.

Murmur consists of two identical syllables, *mur* and *mur*. Compare *murmur* with the word *summer*.

Miscellaneous Words

annexation	ăn nĕx ā′ tion	act of adding or joining.
basket	bȧs′ kĕt	container made of woven twigs.
certainty	çēr′ taĭn tў	quality of being sure.
cessation	çĕs sā′ tion	pause; stopping; intermission.
conclusion	eŏn elụ′ sion (zhŭn)	end; inference; last part.
consummate	eŏn′ sŭm māte	bring to the highest point.
degradation	dĕg rȧ dā′ tion	act of lowering in rank.
deplorable	dĕ plōr′ ȧ ble	lamentable; causing grief.
emanate	ĕm′ ȧ nāte	proceed from a source.
familiar	fȧ mĭl′ iar (yȧr)	friendly; well-known.
forgotten	fŏr gŏt′ ten	left behind through oversight.
gigantic	gī găn′ tĭe	huge; enormous; colossal.
impossibility	ĭm pŏs sĭ bĭl′ ĭ tў	that which cannot be done.
indefinite	ĭn dĕf′ ĭ nĭte	vague; uncertain; not exact.
indicate	ĭn′ dĭ eāte	show; suggest; point out.
inform	ĭn fôrm′	give definite information.
insufficient	ĭn′ sŭf fĭ cient (shĕnt)	not enough for the purpose.
intention	ĭn tĕn′ tion	object; purpose; import.
investigate	ĭn vĕs′ tĭ gāte	inquire into very carefully.
malicious	mȧ lĭ′ cious (shŭs)	spiteful; having ill will.
manufacture	măn ụ̆ făe′ tụ̆re	make from raw materials.
original	ŏ rĭg′ ĭ năl	first in order; not copied.
prejudice	prĕj′ ụ dĭçe	unreasonable bias; dislike.
scuttle	seŭt′ tle	pail for carrying coal.
superstructure	sū pēr strŭe′ tụ̆re	upper part of a building.

Refer to a dictionary for definition, pronunciation, and use of:

nervous,   revival,   syringe,   therefore,   wondering.

In the treatment of silent letters it will be observed that the letter *a* is silent in a large number of words; as in *bread, read, each, goat, heat, head, realm, teach.* Compile an additional list of similar words.

Further and *farther* are sometimes confused although some writers make no distinction. *Further* is understood to refer to time, quantity, or degree, and *farther* has to do with distance.

Miscellaneous Words

apprentice	ăp prĕn′ tĭçe	one learning a trade.
appropriation	ăp prō prĭ ā′ tion	money set apart for a purpose.
beginning	bĕ gĭn′ nĭng	origin; starting place.
connivance	eŏn nīv′ ănçe	voluntary oversight.
correction	eŏr rĕe′ tion	rectification; amendment; rebuke.
existence	ĕx ĭst′ ĕnçe	state of being; reality.
flimsy	flĭm′ sў	weak; unsubstantial; thin.
guidance	guīd′ ănçe	supervision; direction.
imbecile	ĭm′ bĕ çĭle	idiotic; feeble-minded.
inconsistent	ĭn eŏn sĭst′ ĕnt	contradictory; changeable.
inebriate	ĭn ē′ brĭ āte	habitual drunkard.
invitation	ĭn vĭ tā′ tion	request for a person or person's company.
lamentable	lăm′ ĕn tȧ ble	sorrowful; miserable; mournful.
perennial	pĕr ĕn′ nĭ ăl	perpetual; lasting year after year.
prominent	prŏm′ ĭ nĕnt	noticeable; distinguished.
raffle	răf′ fle	form of lottery.
readily	rĕad′ ĭ lў	willingly; promptly.
regard	rĕ gärd′	esteem; respect; consideration.
remember	rĕ mĕm′ bĕr	retain in mind; recall; recollect.
renovate	rĕn′ ŏ vāte	restore; make new again.
ruffian	rŭf′ fĭ ăn	brute; boisterous fellow.
specific	spĕ çĭf′ ĭe	definite; precise.
surveyor	sŭr ve̤y′ ŏr	one who makes measurements.
suspicious	sŭs pĭ′ cious (shŭs)	doubtful; mistrustful.
versatile	vĕr′ sȧ tĭle	able to do many things.

Refer to a dictionary for definition, pronunciation, and use of:

instinct,   irregular,   predecessor,   showing,   usurp.

Note that the letter *d* is silent in *handkerchief, handsome,* and in the first syllable of *Wednesday.* As commonly pronounced, *d* is also silent in *grandmother, grandfather,* and *granddaughter.* Should it be silent according to your dictionary?

G is silent in *assigned, assignment, cologne,* and *gnaw.*

Miscellaneous Words

appointment	ăp point′ mĕnt	engagement for a meeting.
consensus	eŏn sĕn′ sŭs	general agreement of opinion.
considerable	eŏn sĭd′ ẽr à ble	important; notable; large.
defiance	dĕ fī′ ănçe	challenge; scornful disregard.
disconsolate	dĭs eŏn′ sŏ late (ĭt)	sad; filled with grief.
extinguish	ĕx tĭn′ guĭsh	quench; choke; end.
harangue	hà răngue′	noisy, ranting, pompous speech.
inanimate	ĭn ăn′ ĭ māte	listless; without animal life.
insatiable	ĭn sā′ ti à ble (shĭ)	incapable of satisfaction.
instantaneous	ĭn stăn tā′ nĕ oŭs	done at a given instant.
pernicious	pẽr nĭ′ cious (shŭs)	highly injurious or hurtful.
pertinent	pẽr′ tĭ nĕnt	timely; relevant; applicable.
present	prĕṣ′ ĕnt	now, not past or future.
prestige	prĕs tige′ (tezh′)	success or reputation.
privilege	prĭv′ ĭ lĕġe	special favor or advantage.
request	rĕ quĕst′	petition; demand.
research	rĕ sẽarch′	scholarly investigation.
resentment	rĕ ṣĕnt′ mĕnt	displeasure; indignation.
response	rē spŏnse′	reply.
rigid	rĭġ′ ĭd	firm; stiff; inflexible.
saturate	săt u̯ rāte	soak; fill completely.
something	sòme′ thĭng	indefinite amount of anything.
tranquil	trăn′ quĭl	calm and quiet; serene.
wither	wĭth′ ẽr	shrivel; dry.
yellow	yĕl′ lōw	color like that of gold.

Refer to a dictionary for definition, pronunciation, and use of:

cordial,   easel,   pedigree,   precocious,   terminate.

In addition to the previous notation of the use of *g* as a silent letter, it will be noted that it is silent when it precedes *n*; as in *gnat, gnaw, gneiss.* It is also silent before final *m* and *n*; as in *phlegm, condign,* and *sign.*

Giblets, the heart, liver, and gizzard of fowls, are used as food. In Yorkshire a fat man is known as "giblets."

Test is from a Latin word *testum,* meaning an earthen pot used for melting and refining metals.

Miscellaneous Words

arduous	är' dŭ oŭs	exhausting; difficult.
brevity	brĕv' ĭ tў	shortness; terseness.
canoe	eȧ nọe'	small, light boat.
caprice	eȧ prïçe'	fancy; whimsey; humor.
comprehen-	eŏm prẹ hĕn' sĭ ble	understandable; intelligible.
sible		
convenient	eŏn vēn' ient	agreeable; suitable; appropri-
	(yĕnt)	ate.
diverge	dĭ vẽrġe'	extend in different directions.
dubious	dū' bĭ oŭs	doubtful.
exacted	ĕx ăct' ĕd	demanded as a right; compelled.
grateful	grāte' ful	thankful; causing pleasure.
gratify	grăt' ĭ fȳ	satisfy; indulge; to please.
happen	hăp' pĕn	occur, take place.
inflation	ĭn flā' tion	state of being expanded.
juvenile	jụ' vẽ nĭle	youthful.
necessitate	nĕ çĕs' sĭ tāte	impel; oblige.
obnoxious	ŏb nŏx' ious (shŭs)	extremely disagreeable.
occasion	ŏe eȧ' sion (zhŭn)	special event; incident.
odious	ō' dĭ oŭs	repulsive; deserving hatred.
partial	pär' tial (shăl)	not entire; incomplete.
particular	păr tĭe' ŭ lȧr	precise; fastidious; exact.
porous	pō' roŭs	full of minute holes.
position	pŏ ṣĭ' tion	employment; social standing.
replying	rẹ plȳ' ĭng	answering.
tedious	tē' dĭ oŭs	irksome; monotonous.
urgency	ûr' ġĕn çў	insistence; pressure.

Refer to a dictionary for definition, pronunciation, and use of:
hustle,   onerous,   soften,   supersede,   therefore.

Affect and *effect* are often confused through a lack of appreciation of the correct meanings of these two words. Either one may be used as a verb, but *effect* is more commonly used as a noun. *Affect* means "to influence;" as "How does the music affect you?" or "The war will affect the stock market." *Effect* means "to complete, realize, bring about, fulfill;" as "They found it difficult to effect their purpose," or "His reading will effect an improvement in his writing" As a noun, "The effect of the settlement was ruinous."

Miscellaneous Words

alert	à lẽrt′	watchful.
apportion	ăp pōr′ tion	divide into shares or parts.
caricature	eăr′ ĭ eà tу̣re	exaggerated likeness.
casual	eas′ û ăl (kăzh′)	accidental; without design.
derogatory	dĕ rŏg′ à tō rў̆	disparaging; detracting; injurious.
deviate	dē′ vĭ āte	turn aside; divert; vary.
enforce	ĕn fōrçe′	cause to be obeyed; compel.
facilities	fà çĭl′ ĭ tĭeş	means of doing things easily.
gorgeous	gôr′ geous (jŭs)	showy; covered with finery.
heavy	hĕav′ ў̆	weighty; burdensome.
independence	ĭn dĕ pĕnd′ ĕnçe	freedom of action or thought.
influential	ĭn flu̧ ĕn′ tial (shăl)	exerting power or authority.
insurgent	ĭn sûr′ ġĕnt	rising against authority.
obstacle	ŏb′ stà ele	hindrance; obstruction.
precipice	prĕç′ ĭ pĭçe	very steep place or cliff.
presume	prĕ şūme′	taken for granted; suppose.
prevalence	prĕv′ à lĕnçe	widespread usage or acceptance.
principle	prĭn′ çĭ ple	fundamental truth.
propriety	prô prī′ ĕ tў̆	correctness; fitness.
qualities	qu̧al′ ĭ tĭeş	attributes; characteristics.
returned	rĕ tûrn′ ed	sent or brought back; restored.
satisfaction	săt ĭs făe′ tion	contentment; gratification.
splendid	splĕn′ dĭd	magnificent; grand; glorious.
terms	tẽrmş	conditions or stipulations.
terrace	tẽr′ raçe (ĭs)	small, grassy sloping bank.

Refer to a dictionary for definition, pronunciation, and use of:

absolutely,   fracture,   morgue,   patrol,   stamina.

In words ending with *n* or *l* preceded by *e*, the *e* is usually silent; as in *often, glisten,* and *mantel.* Among the exceptions are: *chicken, hyphen,* and *woolen.*

The words *loose* and *lose* are somewhat similar in spelling. This similarity frequently causes confusion. The trouble is not in the spelling but in knowing what these words mean.

Miscellaneous Words

assumption	ăs sŭmp′ tion	something taken for granted.
auspicious	aus pĭ′ cious (shŭs)	favorable; of good omen.
beautiful	beaū′ tĭ fŭl	delightful to the senses.
capacity	eȧ păç′ ĭ tў	ability; what a vessel holds.
copious	eō′ pĭ oŭs	abundant; in great quantities.
disgrace	dĭs grāçe′	shame; dishonor; loss of respect.
flattery	flăt′ tĕr ў	false or insincere praise.
inactivity	ĭn ăe tĭv′ ĭ tў	idleness; inertness.
incorrect	ĭn eŏr rĕet′	faulty; not according to truth.
indulgence	ĭn dŭl′ ġĕnçe	gratification; favor granted.
inspector	ĭn spĕe′ tŏr	examiner; overseer.
obliterate	ŏb lĭt′ ēr āte	destroy by any means; erase.
offer	ŏf′ fēr	proposal; bid; tender.
oppressive	ŏp prĕs′ sĭve	treating with tyranny; severity.
preliminary	prĕ lĭm′ ĭ nar ў (nĕr)	that which goes before.
president	prĕṣ′ ĭ dĕnt	presiding officer.
receptacle	rĕ çĕp′ tȧ ele	vessel used to hold things.
recluse	rĕ eluṣe′	one who lives in seclusion.
rectitude	rĕe′ tĭ tūde	moral uprightness; integrity.
referable	rĕf′ ēr ȧ ble	that which may be referred.
sarcastic	sär eăs′ tĭe	taunting; ironical; scornful.
subsequent	sŭb′ sĕ quĕnt	following or coming after.
tendency	tĕn′ dĕn çў	direction or inclination; trend.
transfer	trăns fēr′	move from one to another.
viaduct	vī′ ȧ dŭet	high bridge with short spans.

Refer to a dictionary for definition, pronunciation, and use of:

constancy, preclude, pungency, purchase, quadruple.

The letter *d* is silent before *g* in the same syllable; as *hedge*, *budget*, and *fidget*. The combined letters *dd* are usually pronounced with a single sound; as *add*, *odd*, and others.

The suffix *ful* (meaning "full of") is never spelled with two *l's*. However if *ly* is added to the suffix, two *l's* will be required.

"A sharp tongue is the only edged tool that grows keener with constant use."

Miscellaneous Words

access	ăc′ çĕss	means of approach; entrance.
approximate	ăp prŏx′ ĭ mate (mĭt)	nearly accurate or correct.
beneficial	bĕn′ ĕ fī′ cial (fĭsh ăl)	useful; fitted to do good.
celebrity	çĕ lĕb′ rĭ tў	noted or distinguished person.
chagrin	çhà grĭn′	feeling of disappointment.
coincide	eō ĭn çīde′	agree at all points.
colossal	eŏ lŏs′ săl	gigantic; of very great size.
conversant	eŏn′ vēr sănt	familiar; acquainted.
discreet	dĭs ereēt′	show good judgment; not rash.
foundry	found′ rў	place where metals are cast.
impostor	ĭm pŏs′ tōr	pretender; deceiver.
innovation	ĭn nŏ vā′ tion	novelty; something new.
maintenance	māin′ tĕ nănçe	means of support; livelihood.
overdue	ō′ vēr dūe	due sometime ago; delayed.
pitiless	pĭt′ ĭ lĕss	having no sympathy; merciless.
proposal	prŏ pōs̝′ ăl	offer; proposition.
pursue	pur sūe′ (pēr)	chase; follow after; hunt.
recede	rĕ çēde′	fall back; move back or away.
referred	rĕ fērred′	submitted for consideration.
segregate	sĕg′ rĕ gāte	set apart; separate from others.
stupendous	stŭ pĕn′ doŭs	astonishing in size or force.
submitted	sŭb mĭt′ tĕd	gave in or yielded.
together	to gĕth′ ēr	in company or union; in concert.
transferable	trăns fēr′ à ble	able to be transferred.
vexation	vĕx ā′ tion	state of being troubled.

Refer to a dictionary for definition, pronunciation, and use of:

amiable,   ridiculous,   separator,   spirit,   vibrate.

Words with *all* are written as two words; as, *all right, all ways, all together*. *Already* (as one word) means "prior to some specified time." "He has reported already." But "We are all ready to fill your order." *Altogether* as one word means in "one piece or unit." *All together* as two words means everybody in one group; as, "They arrived all together."

Miscellaneous Words

affable	ăf′ fà ble	agreeable in speech or manners.
amazement	à māze′ mĕnt	causing astonishment; wonder.
appreciate	ăp prē′ ci āte (shĭ)	value highly; esteem.
dilapidated	dĭ lăp′ ĭ dāt ĕd	fallen into decay or disuse.
disappoint	dĭs ăp point′	defeat the hope of expectation.
dismal	dĭz̧′ măl	gloomy; dreary; cheerless.
enthusiastic	ĕn thū z̧ĭ ăs′ tĭe	ardent; filled with zeal.
estimable	ĕs′ tĭ mà ble	worthy of great respect.
humiliate	hŭ mĭl′ ĭ āte	shame or degrade; mortify.
lubricate	lū′ brĭ eāte	apply oil to lessen friction.
nuisance	nūi′ sănçe	something very troublesome.
promiscuous	prŏ mĭs′ eŭ oŭs	grouped without order; mixed.
promised	prŏm′ ised (ĭst)	pledged to do something.
random	răn′ dȯm	lack of method; aimless.
sediment	sĕd′ ĭ mĕnt	matter deposited at the bottom.
solitary	sŏl′ ĭ tar y̆ (tĕr)	all alone; apart from others.
subserve	sŭb sērve′	serve in a minor capacity.
supreme	sŭ prēme′	highest in rank or authority.
toward	tō′ wărd	in the direction of.
ultra	ŭl′ trà	excessively great; extreme.
until	ŭn tĭl′	up to the time that; till.
valise	và lïse′	leather traveling bag.
venerable	vĕn′ ĕr à ble	worthy of meriting honor.
vicinity	vĭ çĭn′ ĭ tў	nearness; neighborhood.
visionary	vi′ sion ar y	
	(vĭzh′ ŭn ĕr ĭ)	dreamy; not practicable.

Refer to a dictionary for definition, pronunciation, and use of:

decorum,   irreparable,   purpose,   surname,   venom.

When the letter *h* is the first letter of a word, it is silent in a few instances; as, *heir, honor, honest, herb,* and *hour.* At one time it was silent in *hostler, humble,* and *humor.* It is now aspirated. It is not silent in *Durham* or in *humbug.*

The letter *k* is silent when it occurs before the letter *n*; as, *knell, knife, knot, knowledge, knee,* and *knuckle.* Increase the list.

Miscellaneous Words

abandon	à băn′ dŏn	forsake utterly; give up.
antiquated	ăn′ tĭ quāt ĕd	old-fashioned; out-of-date.
aperture	ăp′ ĕr t̯ṳre	opening; hole; passage.
chaperon	ҫhăp′ ĕr ōn	protector for young ladies.
cigarette	ҫĭg à rĕtte′	tobacco rolled in thin paper.
delible	dĕl′ ĭ ble	erasable; removable.
frigid	frĭg′ ĭd	very cold; stiff and formal.
incessant	ĭn ҫĕs′ sănt	without interruption.
inseparable	ĭn sĕp′ à rà ble	incapable of being disjoined.
irrespective	ĭr rĕ spĕe′ tĭve	regardless; without regard.
languish	lăŋ′ guish (gwĭsh)	become dull; pine away.
lineament	lĭn′ ē à mĕnt	outline of one's features.
mitigate	mĭt′ ĭ gāte	make or become less severe.
mutilate	mū′ tĭ lāte	maim; disfigure; cripple.
nutriment	nū′ trĭ mĕnt	food; nourishment; sustenance.
observant	ŏb ṣĕr′ vănt	watchful; taking notice.
previous	prē′ vĭ oŭs	going before in point of time.
program	prō′ grăm	plan of procedure.
sullen	sŭl′ lĕn	unsociable; showing ill humor.
syllable	sўl′ là ble	part of a word.
tentative	tĕn′ tà tĭve	based on a trial; experimental.
urgent	ûr′ ğĕnt	needing immediate attention.
variable	vā′ rĭ à ble	changeable.
vigorous	vĭg′ ŏr oŭs	full of strength; energetic.
western	wĕst′ ĕrn	pertaining to the west.

Refer to a dictionary for definition, pronunciation, and use of:

irregular,   ludicrous,   purpose,   ridicule,   truly.

Synonyms discriminated. Abolish means "to do away with entirely."
Suppress is "to check or restrain;" as, to suppress a yawn. *Cancel* is "to annul or strike out." It may refer to an invitation, a check, a request, or an operation in arithmetic. *Revoke* means in a general way to recall; as, to revoke a license. A *repeal* pertains to revoking a law, and *countermand* pertains to recalling an order for goods.

Miscellaneous Words

annihilate	ăn nī′ hĭ lāte	destroy entirely; wipe out.
appertain	ăp pẽr tāin′	belonging by right; relate.
atrocious	ȧ trō′ cious (shŭs)	extremely cruel or wicked.
carton	cär′ tŏn	box made of pasteboard.
coalesce	cō ȧ lĕsce′	unite or form into one body.
collector	cŏl lĕe′ tŏr	one who collects for another.
curiosity	cū rĭ ŏs′ ĭ tў	something strange or rare.
destitution	dĕs tĭ tū′ tion	state of extreme poverty.
discernible	dĭş cẽrn′ ĭ ble	visible; apparent.
eccentric	ĕe çĕn′ trĭe	acting in a strange way; odd.
element	ĕl′ ĕ mĕnt	first or main principle.
emigrate	ĕm′ ĭ grāte	leave a country.
facilitate	fȧ çĭl′ ĭ tāte	make easier or less difficult.
happen	hăp′ pĕn	occur by chance.
immigrate	ĭm′ mĭ grāte	enter a country.
miniature	mĭn′ ĭ ȧ tu̢re	very small copy; diminutive.
optimist	ŏp′ tĭ mĭst	one who looks for the best.
ostensible	ŏs tĕn′ sĭ ble	apparent; offered as genuine.
private	prī′ vate (vĭt)	personal; secret; not public.
typical	tўp′ ĭ căl	representative of a class.
unfortunate	ŭn fôr′ tu̢ năte	not prosperous; unsuccessful.
usage	ūs′ age (ĭj)	long-continued custom.
variety	vȧ rī′ ĕ tў	mixture of different things.
vestige	vĕs′ tĭge	something left or remaining.
villain	vĭl′ lain	one capable of a great crime.

Refer to a dictionary for definition, pronunciation, and use of:

intelligible,   quality,   quiet,   rating,   superb.

Among the silent letters *l* is silent in *alms, almond, balk, calm, chalk, could, talk,* and many others.

Some letters are never silent in the English language. They are: *f, j, q, r, v, x,* and the letters represented by the sound *sh*.

The dictionary is the geography of human knowledge.

—McKnight.

LESSON 155

Miscellaneous Words

affiliate	ăf fĭl′ ĭ āte	be intimately associated.
amenable	à mē′ nà ble	easy to be led or influenced.
appreciative	ăp prē′ ci ā tĭve (shĭ)	showing grateful regard.
audacious	au dā′ cious (shŭs)	very daring or bold; impudent.
competent	cŏm′ pĕ tĕnt	capable; fitted or able to do.
derision	dĕ rĭ′ sion (zhŭn)	mockery; scorn.
dispensable	dĭs pĕn′ sà ble	not binding.
especially	ĕs pĕ′ cial lў (shăl)	particularly; chiefly.
festival	fĕs′ tĭ văl	time of rejoicing; celebration.
germicide	ġĕr′ mĭ çīde	that which destroys germs.
hoeing	hōe′ ĭng	using a hoe with which to till.
intricate	ĭn′ trĭ cate (kĭt)	exceedingly complicated.
locomotion	lō cŏ mō′ tion	moving from place to place.
morning	môrn′ ĭng	early part of the day.
mourning	mōurn′ ĭng	expression or sign of grief.
practice	prăc′ tĭçe	drill.
propel	prŏ pĕl′	push or drive forward.
reservoir	rĕṣ′ ēr voir (vwôr)	place for collecting water.
specialty	spĕ′ cial tў (shăl)	distinctive mark or quality.
successor	sŭc çĕs′ sŏr	one who succeeds another.
suggestion	sŭg ġĕs′ tion (chŭn)	something proposed; a hint.
tomorrow	tọ mŏr′ rōw	day after today.
triplicate	trĭp′ lĭ cate	threefold; triple.
vegetarian	vĕġ ē târ′ ĭ ăn	one who lives on plant food.
venomous	vĕn′ ŏm ous	full of spite or poison.

Refer to a dictionary for definition, pronunciation, and use of:

congratulate, identify, incidence, incidental, lacerate.

Dele is a term used in printing. It means "to mark for omission something typed or written." It is from the Latin *deleo*, meaning "to destroy."

Stet is another term used in printing, signifying that something once marked for omission is to remain. Briefly, it means "let it stand." It is a kingly edict, "Let it live."

Geo is from the Greek and signifies the earth, ground, or soil, when combined with other forms. *Graph* is "to write or describe"; hence, *geography* is a description of the earth.

144

Miscellaneous Words

adulterate	à dŭl′ tẽr āte	mix with inferior material.
consciousness	eŏn′ scious nĕss (shŭs)	state of mental activity.
detriment	dĕt′ rĭ mĕnt	that which injures or hurts.
enhance	ĕn hȧnçe′	increase in price or worth.
excellent	ĕx′ çĕl lĕnt	superior; of great value.
exquisite	ĕx′ quĭ ṣīte	of fine quality; excellent.
grandeur	grăn′ deͧr	splendor of appearance.
immense	ĭm mĕnse′	very large; huge; enormous.
notify	nō′ tĭ fȳ	make known; inform; acquaint.
nullify	nŭl′ lĭ fȳ	make null; repeal; cancel.
often	ôf′ tĕn	many times; very frequently.
omit	ŏ mĭt′	leave out.
ordinary	ôr′ dĭ nar ȳ (nĕr)	commonplace; customary; usual.
ought	ôught	expedient or imperative; aught.
patronage	pā′ tròn age (ĭj)	trade given to a merchant.
peaceable	pēaçe′ à ble	gentle; not quarrelsome.
probably	prŏb′ à blȳ	more than likely.
prompt	prŏmpt	ready and quick to act.
scarcity	seâr′ çĭ tȳ	state of being scant; dearth.
sensible	sĕn′ sĭ ble	reasonable; wise or prudent.
smiling	smīl′ ĭng	looking pleasant or joyful.
sobriety	sŏ brī′ ĕ tȳ	gravity of manner; moderation.
successful	sŭe çĕss′ fu̧l	prosperous; fortunate.
undoubtedly	ŭn doubt′ ĕd lȳ	without a question.
warehouse	wâre′ house	building used for storing goods.

Refer to a dictionary for definition, pronunciation, and use of:
decorus,   embezzle,   germination,   nepotism,   remiss.

There is a distinction between *embezzlement* and *larceny*. *Larceny* is the wrongful taking and carrying away of the goods, money, or property belonging to another with the intent to convert it to the use of the taker, without the lawful consent of the owner.

Embezzlement is a breach of trust. It is the wrongful appropriation of money or personal property by one who came into its possession rightfully and afterward converted it to his own use.

Miscellaneous Words

applicant	ăp′ plĭ eănt	candidate for a position.
aspirant	ăs pīr′ ănt	eager seeker after honors.
ceremony	çĕr′ ĕ mō nў	sacred right or formality.
clamor	elăm′ ŏr	loud and continuous noise.
confiscate	eŏn′ fĭs eāte	take for public use.
degenerate	dĕ ğĕn′ ĕr āte	become inferior in quality.
dissuade	dĭs suade′ (swād′)	give advice against.
eliminate	ĕ lĭm′ ĭ nāte	get rid of; leave out.
enmity	ĕn′ mĭ tў	ill will; hatred; hostility.
exploit	ĕx ploit′	put to use selfishly.
fascinate	făs′ çĭ nāte	charm; hold by a spell.
judicious	jụ dĭ′ cious (shŭs)	according to sound judgment.
kerosene	kĕr′ ŏ sēne	light-giving oil.
observation	ŏb sĕr vā′ tion	state of being observed.
peculiar	pĕ eūl′ iar (yȧr)	odd; not common to many.
perfect	pĕr′ fĕet	without flaw; lacking nothing.
permission	pĕr mĭs′ sion	consent of one in authority.
positively	pŏṣ′ ĭ tĭve lў	very explicitly; really.
precious	prĕ′ cious (shŭs)	costly; of very great value.
precision	prĕ çĭ′ sion (zhŭn)	state of being very exact.
prudence	prụ′ dĕnçe	carefulness in thought.
sacrifice	săe′ rĭ fīçe	give up at a personal loss.
sagacious	sȧ gā′ cious (shŭs)	wise; not easily deceived.
servitude	sĕr′ vĭ tūde	bondage; menial employment.
undivided	ŭn dĭ′ vīd′ ĕd	whole; not separated.

Refer to a dictionary for definition, pronunciation, and use of:
anxiety, canard, sagacity, stagger, unusual.

There are many peculiar place names. *Peculiar* in Cass county, Missouri, is one of them. When a postoffice was established at this place, the citizens seeking a name to adorn with dignity the new place asked the advice of the Post Office Department in Washington. They informed the official to whom they wrote that they wanted an outstanding name, something to grip the imagination and stick to the memory—something "peculiar." The letter was returned to the committee with a mark around the word "Peculiar," with the notation, "There you are," written on the margin. And it has been Peculiar ever since.

Miscellaneous Words

alleviate	ăl lē′ vĭ āt*e*	relieve; make easier.
assume	ăs sūm*e*′	take for granted; pretend.
cautious	ea̧*u*′ tious (shŭs)	using great care; watchful.
crevice	erĕv′ ĭç*e*	small narrow opening; fissure.
distort	dĭs tôrt′	twist out of shape; pervert.
elicit	ė̇ lĭç′ ĭt	draw out bit by bit.
embarrass	ĕm băr′ răss	involve in trouble; confuse.
essential	ĕs sĕn′ tial (shăl)	indispensable; most important.
fictitious	fĭe tĭ′ tious (shŭs)	not true or real; imaginary.
fissure	fĭs′ sur*e* (fĭsh ēr)	crack, cleft, or split.
frivolous	frĭv′ ŏ loŭs	not serious; of little worth.
funeral	fū′ nĕr ăl	burial ceremony or procession.
history	hĭs′ tŏ rў	account of past events.
illicit	ĭl lĭç′ ĭt	not allowed by law; improper.
interpret	ĭn tēr′ prĕt	explain or tell the meaning.
liberal	lĭb′ ēr ăl	giving freely; open-minded.
merriment	mĕr′ rĭ mĕnt	mirth; fun and laughter.
mysterious	mўs tē′ rĭ oŭs	not clearly understood.
perforate	pĕr′ fŏ rāt*e*	pierce; make a hole through.
pitiful	pĭt′ ĭ fu̧l	sad or tender-hearted.
portion	pōr′ tion	limited part of anything.
prepared	prĕ pâr*e*d′	fitted out for a purpose.
sanguine	săŋ′ gu̧in*e* (gwĭn)	inclined to be hopeful.
spurious	spū′ rĭ oŭs	false; counterfeit; not real.
temporary	tĕm′ pŏ rar ў (rĕr)	lasting for a limited time.

Refer to a dictionary for definition, pronunciation, and use of:

coinage, conduct, intermittent, obstinate, perverseness.

Following a consonant at the end of a syllable, the letter *e* is usually silent. Its purpose is to indicate that the preceding vowel is long; as *came* not *cam*, *tone* not *ton*, *dime* not *dim*. Like all other rules this one has exceptions as illustrated by the use of *one*, *examine*, *none*, and others.

At the beginning of a syllable or word, the letter *u* is used as a consonant. At the end of a word or in the middle of a word or syllable, it is used as a vowel.

Miscellaneous Words

ability	à bĭl′ ĭ tў	power to do something.
abyss	à bўss′	deep immeasurable space, chasm, or void.
accede	ăe çēde′	comply; agree or yield.
accident	ăe′ çĭ dĕnt	something entirely unexpected.
acme	ăe′ mĕ	highest point; culmination.
acute	à eūte′	intense; sharp-pointed.
agility	à ġĭl′ ĭ tў	moving easily or quickly.
agitate	ăġ′ ĭ tāte	disturb; shake up or stir.
allude	ăl lūde′	hint at; refer to indirectly.
amendment	à mĕnd′ mĕnt	change for the better.
appall	ăp pạll′	frighten or fill with horror.
charity	chăr′ ĭ tў	generosity to the poor.
consistent	eŏn sĭs′ tĕnt	not self-contradictory.
discretion	dĭs erĕ′ tion	prudence; wise judgment.
expel	ĕx pĕl′	drive out; send away by force.
gratis	grā′ tĭs	freely and without charge.
hostile	hŏs′ tĭle	unfriendly; showing ill will.
insect	ĭn′ sĕet	small, usually winged animal.
insistence	ĭn sĭst′ ĕnçe	act of persisting; urgency.
negligent	nĕg lĭ′ ġĕnt	guilty of carelessness; lax.
outrageous	out rā′ ġeoŭs	without regard for decency.
stewardess	stew′ ărd ĕss	woman who attends passengers.
technician	tĕeh nĭ′ cian (shŭn)	one skilled in expert details.
tenable	tĕn′ à ble	defendable.
virulent	vĭr′ ũ lĕnt	exceedingly poisonous.

Refer to a dictionary for definition, pronunciation, and use of:

bass, epitome, impetus, intangible, inexperience.

The letter *q* in English is always followed by the letter *u*. This is true whether it occurs in the initial, medial, or final syllable; as in *queer, queen, question, equal, liquid, antique,* and *grotesque.* These letters are sometimes called twin letters. They have the combined sound of *kw.*

When the termination *ing* is used in forming derivatives from words ending in *ie,* the *e* is usually dropped and the *i* is changed to *y.* This prevents two *i's* coming together as *die, dying; tie, tying; lie, lying;* and others.

Miscellaneous Words

allocate	ăl' lŏ cāte	assign; apportion.
apparently	ăp păr' ĕnt lў	seemingly; evidently.
changeable	chānge à ble	subject to alteration.
clarify	¢lăr' ĭ fȳ	make clear.
conspicuous	¢ŏn spĭe' ủ oŭs	very noticeable; outstanding.
controlled	¢ŏn trōlled'	regulated; curbed.
dietitian	dī ĕ tĭ' tiăn (tĭsh)	one versed in dietetics.
energetic	ĕn ēr ġĕt' ĭe	forceful; vigorous.
flexibility	flĕx ĭ bĭl' ĭ tȳ	adaptability.
hospitality	hŏs pĭ tăl' ĭ tȳ	hospitable treatment or reception.
impartial	ĭm pär' tial (shăl)	fair; unbiased.
indefatigable	ĭn dĕ făt' ĭ gà ble	untiring.
ingenuity	ĭn ġĕ nū' ĭ tȳ	originality.
interfering	ĭn tēr fēr' ĭng	intervening; take part in concerns of others.
liquefy	lĭq' uĕ fȳ	reduce to liquid state.
maneuver	mà neụ' vēr	skillful move.
obsolescence	ŏb sŏ lĕs' ¢ĕn¢e	state of being out-of-date.
occasionally	ŏe ¢ā sion ăl lȳ (zhŭn)	infrequently.
paraphernalia	păr à phēr nā' lĭ à	apparatus; equipment.
pedagogical	pĕd à gŏġ' ĭ ¢ăl	concerned with education.
phenomenal	phĕ nŏm' ĕ năl	extraordinary; unusual.
recapitulation	rē ¢à pĭt ụ lā' tion	concise summary.
reimburse	rē ĭm bûrse'	repay.
solely	sōle' lȳ	alone.
usable	ūṣ' à ble	convenient for use.

Refer to a dictionary for definition, pronunciation, and use of:

interpose, phenomenon, recant, recess, solemnity.

Words discriminated. Command, order, direct, instruct. A ship's captain *commands.* The farmer *orders* the hunter off his land. A teacher *directs* the study of his students. A teacher may *instruct* his students in the art of speaking.

PART III

Appendix

"A man is rich in proportion to what he can do without."

—Thoreau.

A Review and Testing List of Words*

abbreviation
absence
absent
abstract
abstracter
accept
acceptable
access
accessible
accommodate
accommodation
accompanying
accrue
accumulate
accumulation
accumulative
accurate
achievement
acknowledge
acknowledgment
acquaintance
acquiesce
acrimonious
across
adaptable
additional
adequate
adhered
adjacent
admissible
advertisement
advice
advisable
advise

affect
affidavit
affiliate
aggravate
aggression
agricultural
alcohol
allocate
allotted
all right
almanac
already
alter
aluminum
amendment
amicable
among
amortize
amount
analogous
analyses
analysis
analyze
analyzing
anneal
annoyance
answer
antecedent
anxiety
apartment
aperture
apologize
apparently

appearance
appendicitis
application
appointment
apposite
appreciate
appropriate
approximate
apropos
argument
arithmetical
arrangement
article
ascertain
aspirin
assessed
assessment
assets
assignment
assimilated
assured
attach
auspice
authoritative
availability
awkward
bailment
balance
balloon
barrel
battalion
believe
beneficial

*The review and testing words in this and the following lessons were compiled from a list of words submitted by a large and select group of business men in different parts of the United States, representing various occupations. The lists were sent in response to a request for words frequently misspelled by stenographers and other office employees. The words in italics do not appear elsewhere in this text.

A Review and Testing List of Words

beneficiary
benefited
bona fide
brief
brochure
bulletin
business
busses
calcimine
calculation
calendar
calender
calipers
campaign
cancel
canceled
canceling
cancellation
canvass
capital
Capitol
carat
carburetor
carton
casein
casual
catalog
cellulose
certificate
chafe
changeable
chargeable
chauffeur
chief

choose
chose
chute
Cincinnati
circuit
cite
clarify
clearance
cleat
clerk
clinch
collaborate
collectible
collision
commensurate
commiseration
commission
commitment
commodity
communication
complementary
complimentary
conceive
concise
concisely
conclusion
concurrent
condenser
confidential
congested
conscienceless
conscientious
conscientiously

consensus
consideration
consistent
conspicuous
consummate
continually
continuing
continuously
controlled
controversy
convenience
converter
conveyance
co-operate
copy
correct
correspondence
correspondent
corrosion
council
counsel
coupon
courtesies
credence
criticism
criticize
cupola
deceive
decision
definite
definitely
definition
delegate

Refer to a dictionary for definition, pronunciation, and use of:

caisson,   **cite,**   **collusion,**   **connoisseur,**   **alkali.**

A Review and Testing List of Words

delinquent
deliver
dependents
depositary
depository
depression
description
desecrated
desiccated
desirable
deteriorate
devisable
devise
dietitian
dilapidate
diligent
diminish
dining
disappoint
discernible
disciplinary
discrepancy
discriminate
disposing
dissatisfied
distributor
dummy
ecstasy
effect
efficacious
efficient
efficiently
eligible
eliminate

emanates
embarrass
embarrassing
eminent
emphasis
employ
enclosed
enclosure
encyclopedia
energetic
enforceable
equalization
equipment
equipped
equity
equivalent
erosion
escrow
etiquette
evidently
exaggerate
examine
except
exemplary
exhibition
exhilarate
existence
exorbitant
expedite
expense
explanatory
extension
facility

familiar
farther
February
fiduciary
financially
flexibility
fluctuate
forcible
foreclosure
foreign
foremost
forfeit
forty
fraudulent
freight
friend
fulfill
fundamental
further
garnishee
gasoline
gauge
glimpse
grammar
grantee
grantor
grateful
group
guarantee
guarantor
guaranty
happen
harass

Refer to a dictionary for definition, pronunciation, and use of:

inclosure,   inclosed,   imminent,   employe,   employee.

A Review and Testing List of Words

heavier
heifer
height
hence
hireling
hospitality
hypothecate
identity
illegibility
illiterate
immensely
impartial
imperative
inaugurate
incidence
incident
inconvenience
indebted
indefatigable
indefinitely
indemnity
independence
independent
indorsement
inexplicable
inflamed
inflammable
ingenuity
inimical
initial
initiation
innumerable
insistence
installation

installment
insulation
insurable
interfere
interference
interfering
irremediable
irresistible
issuing
isthmus
itemize
jeopardize
judgment
khaki
kimono
label
laboratory
lathe
lean
legislation
legislature
leisure
lenient
lens
license
lieutenant
likelihood
liquefy
livelihood
loneliness
loose
mailable
maintain

maintenance
management
managerial
maneuver
manual
mathematical
maturity
medal
menace
merchandise
metallic
mimeograph
minimum
miscellaneous
misinterpreted
misspell
molded
mortgage
naphtha
navigability
necessary
necessitate
negligence
negligible
neighbor
nickel
niece
nineteenth
ninety
ninth
noticeable
notoriety
nuisance

Refer to a dictionary for definition, pronunciation, and use of:

lose, malleable, meddle, obsolete, interchangeability.

A Review and Testing List of Words

numerous
obsolescence
occasion
occasional
occasionally
occur
occurred
occurrence
occurring
omission
omitted
operative
opposite
optimist
optimistic
option
organization
pamphlet
paraffin
parallel
paralysis
paralyze
paraphernalia
particular
passed
pasteurize
peaceable
pedagogical
pennant
performance
period
permanent
permeate
permissible

personnel
persuade
pertinent
phases
phenomenal
Philippines
picnicking
Pittsburgh
poison
positive
possibility
practice
practitioner
precede
precedent
predecessor
preferable
preferred
premium
prepared
prerogative
prescription
presence
preserve
pressure
prevalent
privilege
probably
procedure
proceed
procured
professional
proficient

promiscuous
proportionately
proprietor
psychological
psychology
purchasable
pursue
quantity
questionnaire
quizzes
rarefy
rarity
realty
recapitulation
receipt
receivable
receive
reciprocate
reciprocity
recommend
recommendation
recurrence
reducible
reference
referred
referring
refinancing
regrettable
reimbursement
remedial
remittance
remitted
remitting

Refer to a dictionary for definition, pronunciation, and use of:

optometry,   quoin,   registrar,   rectitude,   quandary.

A Review and Testing List of Words

repetition	speculation	*therefore*
replies	*speech*	together
reserve	*spotting*	*totaling*
resident	*squeeze*	*tragic*
restrict	*stabilization*	*tranquillity*
resume	*stating*	*transference*
retirement	stationary	*transferred*
rhythm	stationery	transmitter
salable	statistics	*tread*
salesman	strenuous	tremendous
salient	stringency	trolley
San Francisco	*studying*	twelfth
satisfactory	subpoena	*unaccountable*
schedule	*subsidiary*	*unanimously*
Schenectady	*subsidizing*	*uncollectible*
scientifically	succeed	*undesirable*
segregate	*suing*	*unforeseen*
separate	summary	*uniformity*
separately	*summing*	*unprecedented*
separator	*superintend*	until
serviceable .	superintendent	usable
sheriff	supersede	useful
shipment	*supplementary*	validity
shipped	surmise	*varieties*
similar	symmetrical	*versatility*
sincerity	*synonym*	visualize
sizable	syrup	voucher
skillful	tariff	*waived*
solder	*tensile*	warrant
solely	tentative	Wednesday
solicitor	*theoretical*	wharf
sophomore	*theorize*	*wherever*
source	theory	*willful*
speculate		

Refer to a dictionary for definition, pronunciation, and use of:

dominant,   germane,   gesture,   resume,   retrieve.

New Words and Words with New Meanings

acidosis	ăç ĭ dō′ sĭs	form of autointoxication.
addict	ăd′ dĭet	slave to a drug habit.
allergic	ăl lĕr′ ǵĭe	sensitive to some substance.
argyrol	är′ ǵў̆ rōl	eye and throat antiseptic.
arterial	är tē′ rĭ ăl	pertaining to a main highway.
aspirin	ăs′ pĭ rĭn	potent pain-relieving drug.
barrage	bår räge′ (räzh′)	artillery fire barrier.
beautician	beaŭ tĭ′ ciăn (tĭsh)	one who creates loveliness.
blimp	blĭmp	small nonrigid airship.
bloc	blŏe	political or economic group.
bootleg	bo͞ot′ lĕg	obtain by unlawful means.
cellophane	çĕl′ lŏ phāne	thin, moistproof material for wrapping.
chiseler	chĭs′ el ẽr	unfair business schemer.
columnist	eŏl′ ŭm nĭst	writer of a special column in a newspaper.
communism	eŏm′ mŭ nĭ̧sm	theory of common ownership.
compact	eŏm′ păet	lady's first-aid beauty kit.
coverage	eŏv′ ẽr age (ĭj)	assumed insurance risks.
debacle	dĕ bä′ ele	overwhelming disaster.
debunk	dē bŭŋk′	expose insincerity or error.
decelerate	dē çĕl′ ẽr āte	move with decreasing speed.
decode	dē eōde′	translate cipher messages.
depreciable	dĕ prē′ ci à ble (shĭ)	lessening in value.
diathermy	dī′ à thẽr mў̆	curative application of heat electrically applied.
endocrine	ĕn′ dŏ erĭne	any internal secretion.
eugenics	eŭ ǵĕn′ ĭes	science of being well born.

In words, as fashions, the same rule will hold,
Alike fantastic if too new or old;
Be not the first by whom the new are tried,
Nor yet the last to lay the old aside.

—Pope.

Wisdom consisteth not in knowing many things, nor even in knowing them thoroughly; but in choosing and in following what conduces the most certainly to our lasting happiness and true glory.

—Landor.

New Words and Words with New Meanings

Fascism	Făs′ cĭsm (făsh′ ĭzm)	form of state socialism.
fingerprint	fĭn′ gẽr prĭnt	impression of the fingers.
floater	flōat′ ẽr	one without a permanent home.
fundamentalist	fŭn då mĕn′ tăl ĭst	firm believer in the Bible.
gangster	găng′ stẽr	member of a lawless gang.
halitosis	hăl ĭ tō′ sĭs	foul or offensive breath.
high-brow	hīgh′ brow	intellectual or learned snob.
hitchhiker	hĭtch′ hīk ẽr	one who thumbs a free ride.
ideology	ĭd ē ŏl′ ŏ ġy̆	impractical scheme of ideals about life.
insulin	ĭn′ sŭ lĭn	substance retarding diabetes.
intrigue	ĭn trïgue′	plot or plan secretly.
kitchenette	kĭtch ĕn ĕtte′	small room fitted for cooking.
kraft	kråft	dark brown wrapping paper.
legionnaire	lē ġion nâire′ (jŭn)	member of a legion.
lipstick	lĭp′ stĭck	rouge in the form of a stick.
marcel	mär çĕl′	special style of hair waves.
microphone	mī′ erŏ phōne	sound magnifying apparatus.
moron	mō′ rŏn	person of deficient mentality.
mortician	môr tĭ′ ciăn (tĭsh)	professional undertaker.
Nazi	Na′ zï (Nä′ tsĕ)	national socialistic party.
neutral	neū′ trăl	not favoring either side.
novocain	nō vŏ eāin′	general local anesthetic.
overhead	ō vẽr hĕad′	general business operating expenses.
pacifist	păç′ ĭ fĭst	one opposed to military ideals.
panhandle	păn′ hăn dle	solicit alms on the street.

A word fitly spoken is like apples of gold in pictures of silver.

—PROVERBS.

Moratorium is a term applied to a period during which a debtor has a legal right to suspend payment of a debt or other obligation.

A knowledge of words is the gateway of scholarship.

—WILSON.

Lightning, a flash of electricity in the sky. This word has two syllables, *light ning.* Compare with *lightening,* meaning a lessening of weight. How many syllables?

New Words and Words with New Meanings

photostat	phō′ tŏ stăt	camera making direct prints.
plebiscite	plĕb′ ĭ scīte	vote on some special question.
profiteer	prŏf ĭ tēer′	make excessive profits.
pulmotor	pŭl′ mō tŏr	device producing respiration.
purge	pûrḡe	remove political antagonists.
racket	răck′ ĕt	unlawful scheme for extorting money.
racketeer	răck′ ĕt ēer	member of an extortion gang.
radiogram	rā′ dĭ ŏ grăm	message transmitted by radio.
realtor	rē′ ăl tôr	modern real-estate broker.
revue	rĕ vūe′	burlesque of recent events.
robot	rō′ bŏt	mechanically made man.
rodeo	rō′ dĕ ō	exhibition of cowboy life.
sabotage	săb ŏ täḡe′	malicious waste of property.
sanforize	săn fôr īze′	process for shrinking fabrics.
scenario	scĕ nä′ rĭ ō	outline of a photoplay.
soviet	sō vĭ ĕt′	Russian governing body.
speedster	spēed′ stĕr	car capable of great speed.
streamline	strēam′ līne	symmetrical flowing line.
syndicalism	sўn′ dĭ ẹăl ĭşm	revolutionary trades-union.
technology	tĕeh nŏl′ ŏ ḡў	industrial, applied science.
television	tĕl′ ĕ vĭ sion(zhŭn)	transmission by wire of a scene.
totalitarian	tŏ tăl ĭ târ′ ĭ ăn	pertaining to a highly central- ized government.
travelog	trăv′ ĕ lŏg	illustrated lecture on travel.
turnover	tûrn′ ō vĕr	cycles of sales and replace- ments.
unicameral	ū nĭ ẹăm′ ĕr ăl	single legislative body.

Gentlemen's agreement.—This is an informal substitute for an agreement secured upon the honor of parties and is not based upon principles of law. It is understood to be binding upon the participants as a matter of honor. This form of an agreement is usually contrary to some policy of law. Sometimes the parties prove not to be "gentlemen," their word not being as good as "their bond."

Curfew is from two words meaning "cover" and "fire." The cover-fire bell rang at nightfall warning householders to cover or extinguish their fires. No one was then expected to leave his home.

Foreign Nouns and Their Plurals

Singular	Foreign Plurals	English Plurals
LESSON 170	LESSON 171	LESSON 172
apex	apices	apexes
aroma	aromata	aromas
automaton	automata	automatons
axis	axes	axes
basis	bases	bases
beau	beaux	beaus
compendium	compendia	compendiums
crisis	crises	crises
criterion	criteria	criterions
datum	data	data
encomium	encomia	encomiums
executrix	executrices	executrixes
focus	foci	focuses
formula	formulae	formulas
incubus	incubi	incubuses
index	indices	indexes
medium	media	mediums
memorandum	memoranda	memorandums
parenthesis	parentheses	parentheses
radius	radii	radiuses
stratum	strata	stratums
syllabus	syllabi	syllabuses
thesis	theses	theses
vertebra	vertebrae	vertebras
vortex	vortices	vortexes

Refer to a dictionary for the plural form of:

dictum, hypothesis, sinus, synopsis, vertex.

The preferred pronunciation of *data* is dā′ ta. *Data* is the plural of *datum*. The plural form is sometimes used in the singular form; as, "This data has been furnished for your consideration."

Some foreign nouns take either a foreign or an English plural.

Words are the counters of wise men, and the money of fools.

—HOBBS.

Latin Words and Phrases in General Use

ad infinitum ăd ĭn fĭ nī′ tŭm   without end; indefinitely.
anno Domini ăn′ nō Dŏm′ ĭ nī in the year of our Lord.
bona fide bō′ nȧ fī′ dĕ   in good faith; genuine.
caveat emptor ɛā′ vĕ ăt ĕmp′ tôr "let the buyer beware."
de facto dē făɛ′ tō   in fact whether right or not.
ex officio ĕx ŏf fĭ′ ci ō (shĭ) by virtue of an office.
ex parte ĕx pär′ tĕ   one-sided or biased.
ex post facto ĕx pōst făɛ′ tō something done afterwards.
habeas corpus hā′ bĕ ăs ɛôr′ pŭs "you have the body."
in statu quo ĭn stā′ tu̱ quō′   in the same or former state.
in toto ĭn tō′ tō   entirely or completely.
modus operandi mō dŭs ŏ pĕr ăn′ dī manner of operation.
ne plus ultra nē plŭs ŭl′ trȧ utmost perfection.
per annum pĕr ăn′ nŭm   by the year.
per capita pĕr ɛăp′ ĭ tȧ   as individuals; by heads.
per diem pĕr dī′ ĕm   by the day; daily.
per se pĕr sē   through or by itself.
prima facie prī′ mȧ fā ci ē (shĭ) at first view or at sight.
pro rata prō rā′ tȧ   in proportion.
sine die sī′ nĕ dī′ ē   without setting a time.
sine qua non sī′ nē quā nŏn′ indispensable condition.
sub rosa sŭb rō′ s̨ȧ   privately or confidentially.
ultimatum ŭl tĭ mā′ tŭm   final terms offered.
vice versa vī′ cĕ vĕr′ sȧ   in the opposite way.
viva voce vī′ vȧ vō′ çĕ   by word of mouth; orally.

Refer to a dictionary for definition, pronunciation, and use of :

ad valorem,   **alumni,**   **pro tem,**   **verbatim,**   **via.**

Rome, a city in Italy, was founded 752 B. C. Romulus is said to have been the founder. The language of early Rome was Latin. This was the language spoken by the people of Latium, in Italy. The Latin language dominated the school, the church, and the state in western Europe until modern times. As the power of Rome spread, the use of the Latin language increased. The Italian, French, Spanish, and Portugese languages are modified forms of Latin and are called *Romance languages*.

French Words in General Use

a la mode (a la mode'—ä là mōd')[1] "after the fashion."
apropos (ap ro pos'—ăp rŏ pō') to the point.
bagatelle (bag a telle'—băg à tĕl') of no importance; trifle.
blasé (bla se'—blä zā') surfeited with pleasure.
camouflage (eam' ou flage—kăm' ŏŏ fläzh)
     disguise; conceal.
coiffure (eoif fure'—kwä fūr') style of hairdress.
coterie (eo' te rie—kō' tĕ rĭ) certain group of people.
debris (de bris'—dĕ brē') rubbish; litter; fragments.
debut (de but'—dă bū') first public appearance.
denouement (de noue' ment—dā nōō' mäN)
     unraveling of a plot.
éclat (é elat'—å klä') much showiness; renown.
elite (e lite'—å lēt') choice or select social group.
en masse (en masse'—äN mäs') in a body; collectively.
esprit de corps (es prit' de eorps'—ĕs prē 'dē kôr')
     devotion to a cause.
exposé (ex po sé'—ĕks pŏ zā') embarrassing disclosure.
finesse (fi nesse'—fĭ nĕs') artifice or trick; refinement.
naive (nä ïve'—nä ēv') unaffected simplicity.
nonchalance (nŏn' cha lance—nŏN' shà lăNs)
     indifference; unconcern.
passé (pas sé'—pä sā') out-of-date; worn out.
protége (pro' té gé—prō' tà zhä) under the care of another.
regime (re gime'—rå zhēm') system of management.
rendezvous (ren' dez vous—rän' dĕ vōō)
     appointed meeting place.
résumé (re' su mé'—rā zŭ mā') recapitulation; summing up.
table d'hôte (tà ble d'hôte'—tabl' dōt')
     meal of several courses.
trousseau (trous seau'—trōō sō') outfit of a bride.

The small capital letter represents the nasal tone of the preceding vowel, and is made by sending out the breath through both the nose and the mouth, as in *eN route* (aN route). This is common to the French language.

The accent in French differs from the English. In the French language all full syllables are pronounced with equal stress, but there is usually a rising inflection or stress on the last syllable.

---

[1]Words are respelled phonetically to indicate the pronunciation.

States and Territories: Capitals and Large Cities

LESSON 175	LESSON 176	LESSON 177
Alabama (Ala.)	Montgomery	Birmingham
Alaska	Juneau	Nome
Arizona (Ariz.)	Phoenix	Tucson
Arkansas (Ark.)	Little Rock	Fort Smith
California (Calif.)	Sacramento	San Francisco
Colorado (Colo.)	Denver	Pueblo
Connecticut (Conn.)	Hartford	New Haven
Delaware (Del.)	Dover	Wilmington
District of Columbia (D.C.)	Washington	Washington
Florida (Fla.)	Tallahassee	Jacksonville
Georgia (Ga.)	Atlanta	Savannah
Hawaii (H. I.)	Honolulu	Hilo
Idaho	Boise	Pocatello
Illinois (Ill.)	Springfield	Chicago
Indiana (Ind.)	Indianapolis	Evansville
Iowa	Des Moines	Sioux City
Kansas (Kans.)	Topeka	Wichita
Kentucky (Ky.)	Frankfort	Louisville
Louisiana (La.)	Baton Rouge	New Orleans
Maine	Augusta	Bangor
Maryland (Md.)	Annapolis	Baltimore
Massachusetts (Mass.)	Boston	Worcester
Michigan (Mich.)	Lansing	Detroit
Minnesota (Minn.)	St. Paul	Minneapolis
Mississippi (Miss.)	Jackson	Vicksburg
Missouri (Mo.)	Jefferson City	St. Louis

A citizen from Braggadocio, Missouri, compiled a list of the unusual names of towns in that state. Among those that are "unusual" may be listed Cureall, Novelty, and Clever. Out of the regular humdrum will be found Ponder, Competition, and Enough.

Aid is the name of one town, while another is Amity. Rat and Roach are the names of two communities; another is Turtle. Gang and Gentry are two pleasant places; and May and Ink are evidences of the founders' tastes.

Some personal names are taken from the names of local places; as, Ford, Street, Lane, Brook, Bridge, Field, Lake, and Dunn.

States and Territories: Capitals and Large Cities

LESSON 178	LESSON 179	LESSON 180
Montana (Mont.)	Helena	Butte
Nebraska (Nebr.)	Lincoln	Omaha
Nevada (Nev.)	Carson City	Reno
New Hampshire (N. H.)	Concord	Manchester
New Jersey (N. J.)	Trenton	Newark
New Mexico (N. Mex.)	Santa Fe	Albuquerque
New York (N. Y.)	Albany	New York
North Carolina (N. C.)	Raleigh	Charlotte
North Dakota (N. Dak.)	Bismarck	Fargo
Ohio	Columbus	Cleveland
Oklahoma (Okla.)	Oklahoma City	Tulsa
Oregon (Oreg.)	Salem	Portland
Pennsylvania (Pa.)	Harrisburg	Philadelphia
Porto Rico (P. R.)	San Juan	Ponce
Rhode Island (R. I.)	Providence	Pawtucket
South Carolina (S. C.)	Columbia	Charleston
South Dakota (S. Dak.)	Pierre	Sioux Falls
Tennessee (Tenn.)	Nashville	Memphis
Texas (Tex.)	Austin	San Antonio
Utah	Salt Lake City	Ogden
Vermont (Vt.)	Montpelier	Burlington
Virginia (Va.)	Richmond	Norfolk
Washington (Wash.)	Olympia	Seattle
West Virginia (W. Va.)	Charleston	Wheeling
Wisconsin (Wis.)	Madison	Milwaukee
Wyoming (Wyo.)	Cheyenne	Laramie

Alabama is said to derive its name from an Indian tribe. Several different meanings are attributed to the name; as, "burnt clearing;" or "here we rest;" also "thicket clearers."

Alaska is from an Indian word meaning "great country."

Connecticut is from an Indian name, Quonoktacut, meaning a "river whose water is driven in waves by tides or winds."

Manitou is an Indian name given to any object of religious reverence.

Annapolis was so named in honor of Queen Anne, wife of James I of England.

Names of American Cities Difficult to Spell

LESSON 181	LESSON 182	LESSON 183
Aberdeen *Wash*	Hannibal *Mo.*	Paterson *N.J.* *Florida*
Akron *Ohio*	Haverhill *Mass*	Pensacola
Allegheny *Penna.*	Hoboken *N.J.*	Piqua —
Altoona *"*	Holyoke *Mass.*	Pittsburgh *Penn.*
Amsterdam *N.Y.*	Houston *Tex.*	Plymouth *Mass.*
Bayonne *N.J.*	Hutchinson *Kans.*	Portsmouth *N.H.*
Beaumont *Tex.*	Ithaca *N.Y.*	Poughkeepsie *N.Y.*
Berkeley *Calif.*	Joliet *Ill.*	Princeton *N.J.*
Brattleboro	Kalamazoo *Mich.*	Racine *Wis.*
Bridgeport *Conn.*	Kankakee *Ill.*	Roanoke *Virg.*
Brockton *Mass.*	Keokuk *Iowa*	Rochester *Minn.*
Buffalo *N.Y.*	Lafayette *Ind.*	San Diego *Calif.*
Cambridge *Mass.*	Las Vegas *Nev.*	Sandusky *Ohio*
Champaign *Ill.*	Leavenworth *Kans.*	Schenectady *N.Y.*
Chattanooga *Tenn.*	Los Angeles *Calif.*	Scranton *Penna.*
Chautauqua *N.Y.*	Manitou —	Sheboygan *Wis.*
Cincinnati *Ohio*	Mobile *Alabama*	Susquehanna *N.Y.*
Dallas *Tex.*	Moline *Ill.*	Syracuse *N.Y.*
Decatur *Ill.*	Muskegon *Mich.*	Tacoma *Wash.*
Dubuque *Iowa*	Muskogee *Okla.*	Terre Haute *Ind.*
Duluth *Minn.*	Nashua *N.H.*	Trinidad — *Colo.*
Eau Claire *Wisc.*	Niagara *N.Y.*	Valparaiso
Elgin *Ill.*	Norwich *Conn.*	Vancouver *Wash.*
Elkhart *Ind.*	Oconomowoc	Vincennes *Ind.*
El Paso *Texas*	Oneida *N.Y.*	Waukegan *Ill.*
Eugene *Oreg.*	Osawatomie	Waukesha —
Fostoria	Oshkosh *Wis.*	Wilkes-Barre *Penna.*
Galesburg *Ill.*	Ottumwa *Iowa*	Windsor —
Galveston *Tex.*	Paducah *Ky.*	Yakima *Wash*
Gloucester *Mass.*	Pasadena *Calif.*	Ypsilanti

Each of the foregoing cities is noted for some special and distinctive characteristic. Make a notation enumerating some of these special features.

Occupations have been a fruitful source for the origin of names; as, Smith, Goldsmith, Butcher, Carpenter, Miller, Taylor, Hunt and Hunter, Webb and Weaver, Brewer, Baker, and Plummer.

Important Abbreviations and Contractions

adv., advertisement
ad lib., at pleasure
Agt., Agent
amt., amount
assn., association
Asst., Assistant
ave., avenue
bal., balance
bk., book; bank
brt., brought
bu., bushel
cash., cashier
chgs., charges
Co., company
coml., commercial
corp., corporation
Dr., Doctor
doz., dozen
ea., each
e.e., errors excepted
encl., enclosed
e.g., for example
est., established
et al., and others
etc., and so forth
ex., example
f.o.b., free on board
fol., folio
frt., freight
ft., foot
Gov., Governor
gro., gross
id., the same
i.e., that is
inc., incorporated
int., interest

inst., present month
Hon., Honorable
invt., inventory
lab., laboratory
led., ledger
Ltd., limited
L. F., ledger folio
L. S., place of seal
M., one thousand
mdse., merchandise
meas., measure
memo., memorandum
Messrs., Gentlemen
mo., month
mfg., manufacturing
Mr., Mister
mgr., manager
mtg., mortgage
misc., miscellaneous
n.g., no good
No., number
o.e., omissions ex-
    cepted
pd., paid
pcs., pieces
P. O., postoffice
pkg., package
pp., pages
p.p., parcel post
Pres., President
prox., next month
qt., quart
recd., received
Rev., Reverend
R. R., rural route
Sec., Secretary

Sept., September
Sts., Streets
Supt., Superin-
    tendent
tr., transpose
t.b., trial balance
Treas., Treasurer
ult., last month
via, by way of
viz., namely; to wit
vs., against
vol., volume
yd., yard
yr., year
wk., week
wt., weight
%, per cent
c/o, care of
c/f, carried for-
    ward
c/d, carried down
a/c, acct., account
B/L, bill of lading
b/s, bill of sale
¶, paragraph
@, to or at
$, dollars
¢, ct., cent
#, number; pounds
℔, pounds
A1, first class
* * *, an omission
&, and
&c., and so forth
§, section
r, recipe

INDEX

167

INDEX—Concluded